MW00632348

POUL JORGENSEN'S
Favorite Flies
and how to tie them

This book is dedicated to my friend, Preben Torp Jacobsen—
veterinarian, author, artist, entomologist,
Danish fly-fishing guru and teacher.

POUL JORGENSEN'S
Favorite Flies
and how to tie them

POUL JORGENSEN

STACKPOLE
BOOKS

Published by
STACKPOLE BOOKS
5067 Ritter Road
Mechanicsburg, PA 17055
www.stackpolebooks.com

Printed in Denmark

First edition

10 9 8 7 6 5 4 3 2 1

All photos by the author, unless otherwise credited

Poul Jorgensen

Library of Congress Cataloging-in-Publication Data

Jorgensen, Poul.
      Poul Jorgensen's favorite flies: and how to tie them/
Poul Jorgensen.—1st ed.
         p.   cm.
      ISBN 0-8117-0627-3 (hard cover)
      1. Flies, Artificial. 2. Fly tying. I. Title: Favorite flies.
II. Title.
SH451.J642 2000
688.7'9124—dc21

                            99-052545

Contents

Foreword

Flies and fly tying are an unending subject. Since before Izaak Walton's time in the sixteenth century, fishing masters have, in writing and pictures, contributed their experience in the use and construction of our beloved flies.

In several languages, but primarily in English, the contemporary angler and fly tier will find new wisdom concerning fly patterns and tying methods brought about by new tools, hooks, and, most importantly, new materials. Variations in the flies may make some especially suited for certain rivers or countries, depending on the insects found in the area.

It would seem almost unthinkable that a new book about flies and fly tying would give the reader any new knowledge on the subject. Here, however, the world-famous Poul Jorgensen gives the tier guidance in the use and understanding of materials and tying techniques that no other book has covered.

Nearly a half-century ago, I wrote, "In the Middle Ages, learned monks represented the ultimate in education to the people." In that setting, for anglers and fly tiers, Poul Jorgensen would surely be an archbishop.

Svend Saabye
Stenlose, Denmark
April 1999

PHOTO BY MICHAEL JENSEN

Acknowledgments

When the long awaited moment is before you in the form of a mountain of typewritten pages, color slides, letters, and faxes from the publisher telling you that you are way past your deadline, there is a feeling of inner peace that only an author can know. I think back to the days of my childhood, when my father took me fishing, or to the sunny afternoon on Little Diamond Lake north of Chicago where I met the late Bill Blades, the man who started it all and taught me the difference between tying flies and just fly tying.

In my modest library of books by learned authors I have yet to open one which says, "I did it all myself," and this one is no different. So on this page I wish to thank all the anglers and fly tiers with whom I have exchanged ideas, and from whom I have learned a lot. A very special thanks to Larry Solomon who so generously let me use the caddis dry-fly patterns and share them with the rest of our fellow anglers. A heartfelt thanks to

Dr. Jim Gilford of Maryland for letting me use the beautiful photograph of our beloved Green Drake Mayfly in its natural splendor. And to Bill Elliott for the fine drawings of insects found throughout the book. To my publisher and friend Morten Valeur a very special thanks for publishing my books in Danish, and to Martin Hedegaard, who is not only a super fly tier, but also a fine translator without whom this book would have been dead on arrival.

And last but not least, I wish to thank my old friend Lefty Kreh for teaching me to use the camera way back when I needed it, and a very special thanks to Svend Saabye for honoring me with his foreword.

Poul Jorgensen
"Trout Town USA"
Roscoe, New York

Opposite: *An angler on Letort Spring Run in Pennsylvania.*

Chapter 1
Insects and Their
Importance in Fly Fishing

I suppose it's reasonable to assume that in general, insects are regarded as a nuisance by humans. But most of them somehow manage to justify their existence. While the fly fisher may not appreciate all the small creatures that cross his path, he welcomes the sight of flies swarming over his favorite trout water and bringing it to life with leaping and feeding fish. To capitalize on such ideal fishing conditions the angler must identify the insects upon which the fish are feeding and come up with a reasonable artificial.

For the novice this may sound like a mystery. A friend said to me not long ago, "All these discussions about flies, leader tippets, upstream and downstream drift, were hard enough to comprehend, but now that one must learn entomology in order to become a producer of one's own fishing flies I am beginning to think that fly fishing is purposely made difficult and designed for the enjoyment of a few with special talent—and so is fly tying, for that matter." On the contrary, fly fishing can be learned by anyone in a very short time. It is just a way of catching fish under circumstances where other methods are useless or less practical, and, of course, it is a way of enjoying oneself. The fly-tying aspect of the sport is to many much more important than fishing itself. It can be made as simple or as complicated as you want it to be. Anyone who can tie his own shoelaces can learn to tie a fishing fly, provided he is willing to practice. I have never found that I needed a college degree in entomology, and for years I have been able to get by with the knowledge gained by reading articles and books dealing with the subject, and by observing the happenings at streamsides where insects abound. The fly fisher will soon discover that fish will feed on a juicy grasshopper as well as on a tiny midge type of insect that one can't even see. Life in or near the stream or lake covers a wide spectrum of insect species, of which only a very small group is of interest to the angler.

The principal insects dealt with in this book are mayflies, caddisflies, and stoneflies. I also discuss some other less important aquatic species. Within each order of insect there are hundreds of species identified by entomologists, but recorded observations by many dedicated American anglers

An angler collects insects with a little net. These can be stored for later study, providing valuable information about the artificial to use in the water you are fishing.

A handful of collected nymphs.

have narrowed the list to a very few principal hatches, in imitation of which so many fly patterns have been devised.

It is helpful to understand the life cycle of insects. The immature nymph and larva make up a large portion of the fish's diet. In fact, it is estimated that fish consume 85 percent of their food underwater, which explains why a "dry-fly purist" can often get skunked while the nympher is having good fishing. When nymphs are ready to hatch they become very active and are out of hiding in full view of the fish. Before a nymph hatches the skin splits open either underwater, on rocks, or in the surface film, and the winged adult appears. In the case of caddis and stoneflies, no other transformation takes place and they are ready for mating and egg-laying. But the mayfly

undergoes one more change. When it first appears it is known to the angler as a dun. If it manages to escape the fish feasting on a new hatch and flies to safety, it will change into a spinner, usually within twenty-four hours. The fly has now completely changed. The wings are in most cases glossy-clear, and the tails are much longer than those of the dun.

The ability to recognize whether the fish are feeding on the nymph underwater or the emerging nymph in the surface film, or whether they are feeding on the dun or the spinner, is very important not only to the fly fisher, but to the fly tier as well. When the spinners appear over the stream or lake, the mating flight begins. The flies can usually be observed high over the water, often in large swarms. As mating progresses they fly lower and lower, and ultimately the egglaying takes place in the water. The spinners now die, thus ending the life cycle of a precious insect.

During the active period just before or during a hatch, the fish will go wild and the water is often boiling with feeding fish. In most instances the fish become very selective and will feed only on the particular fly hatching at the time. This is perhaps one of the biggest mysteries to many, as it seems quite unreasonable that a fish will refuse a big juicy fly, but be quite willing to gorge on a hatch of tiny midges.

For several years now I have collected some fly specimens every time I went fishing, and needless to say, these specimens have been invaluable as models in my fly-tying efforts. The equipment for starting a collection of insects is relatively inexpensive, or you can make it yourself.

For collecting underwater specimens in riffles or deep fast water, I use a homemade seine consisting of a piece of cheesecloth or window screen suspended between two half-inch dowels. I prefer one large one approximately 3 × 4 feet for heavy-duty work, and one small portable seine 1 × 1 1/2 feet with quarter-inch sticks and cheesecloth so that it can be rolled up and carried in the fishing vest. The seine is operated by standing in the water facing downstream and placing the seine in front of you at an arm's length. It should be spread out and held perpendicular to the stream in a vertical position with the lower edge resting firmly against the stream bottom. Now move rocks and disturb the bottom with your feet, and the nymphs and larvae will be dislodged and carried into the seine by the current. Specimens floating in the surface film can be scooped up with a small aquarium net. I capture flying specimens with a butterfly net that has been modified and fitted with a male ferrule so that it can be mounted on the butt section of my fly rod. Winged specimens can at times be picked up by hand or with small tweezers from their resting places on trees, bushes, and fences near the stream. Some species are attracted by light from a lantern or automobile in the evening, although it is

always best to do the collecting when a hatch is on to assure yourself of getting the right specimens. Since our specimens are to be used as models for the dressing of artificial fishing flies and not for further entomological study, I am satisfied by taking some notes about the color and other characteristics that might be helpful when trying to make positive identification after returning home.

I have talked to many who, like myself, collect a few insects every time they go fishing, and most of us agree that although we have neither the time nor the ambition to become entomologists, it is extremely important to have a collection of basic insect types for use as models in our tying efforts. Not all my fishing friends keep the insects; some merely take notes right at streamside, such as the insect's size, color, and dominating features, which will be helpful to them at a later date. It is best, however, to preserve some specimens in addition to the notes one takes on the spot. Since it is not very practical to pin

A beautiful caddis adult, just hatched. On many waters, the caddis is the most important insect. PHOTO BY MORTEN VALEUR

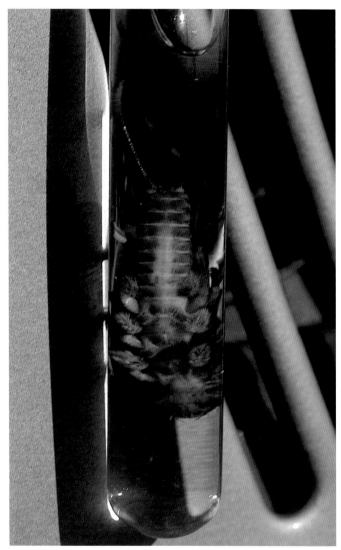

Collected insects can be stored in a tightly-closed container such as a test tube and preserved in a solution of alcohol, glycerin, and white wine vinegar. Attach a small label with information for later reference.

the insects on a board in a dried version because they will eventually deteriorate, I keep them in small glass containers sealed with a tightly fitted cork. Specimens should be kept separate from each other, and there should be no more than a few of the same species together.

There are many different preserving solutions, and I have tried most of them. I presently use a solution consisting of eight parts grain alcohol, one part vinegar, and one part glycerine to prevent the insect from becoming too brittle to handle. Many simply use straight alcohol of 70 to 80 percent strength. Before storing the prepared specimens I label the glass container with the name and where and when it was collected. Some specimens are merely given a number and information pertaining to the specimen is kept on a separate card.

Opposite: *American green drake dun* (Ephemera guttulata). Photo by Jim Gilford

Chapter 2
Materials

The subject of materials has always been a confusing one, at least for someone who is just starting to tie his own flies. I am often asked if there isn't some sort of kit one can buy that has everything in it so we could eliminate all the fussing around looking for the stuff only to end up with a whole room full of more or less useless material. Unfortunately, there is no such kit, and if there were one you would have to stand in line for a long time to get one.

I clearly remember the two items I first owned when I started tying my own flies back in the mid-1950s: a brown rooster neck and razor blade, both given to me by my friend the late Bill Blades. "In case you are wondering what the razor blade is for, I'll tell you," he said while he was looking around on his little tying stand located next to a row of bridge tables full of bottles with lacquer and specimens of insects. "This hook here goes with it, and every time the stuff you put on the hook is not to my liking, the razor blade goes into action." He was not kidding, nor was he kidding about the penny he asked for the hook, a superstitious habit of his. Even though Bill had just moved his tying room from one bedroom to a larger one and had closets full of boxes with material, he still insisted that it's not a lot of material that makes a good fly tier—it's practice!

As I look around in my own tying room I wonder if I forgot to take his advice. However, most of us who have enjoyed the art of fly tying for a number of years know that Bill's reasoning was sound and we have weeded out the unnecessary in favor of just those items which are best suited for the flies we enjoy and will take the most fish.

You will probably find the materials I discuss somewhat strange in comparison with what you are used to, and probably most of the stuff you are acquainted with is not mentioned. Instead, this chapter introduces you to a whole lot of new materials, some formerly thought of as unusable surplus and others that are brand new but particularly adaptable to the flies in this book.

THREAD

Every fly-tying bench has some basic items that are used all the time regardless of what kind of artificials you are dressing. The first that comes to my mind is tying thread, and but a few years ago it was silk, which the tier had to wax and handle with care so as not to fray or break it. Although some of the old-timers still use it, the much stronger prewaxed nylon has become so popular that silk is hard to obtain in some areas. I have used Herb Howard's prewaxed 6/0 thread for some years now and, frankly speaking, I wouldn't know what to do without it since it is all I ever use. It comes in many different colors; if you are a serious fly tier, your bench should never be without black, white, brown, olive, cream, gray, yellow, and orange.

WAX

I still have a lump of special wax that was given to me by Bill Blades, and which sits in the end of an empty wooden thread spool. His recipe was as complicated as the one he used for his basement wine-making and was extremely sticky, which in the days of unwaxed thread was a blessing. Wax is now readily available from your supplier in small pieces and is used for "extra waxing" the thread if needed. I rarely use it except to rub on my fingertips when they get too dry for comfortable working.

CEMENT

There are many different brands of head cement you can get from a supplier, each claiming to be better than the other. For applying on the hook before winding a dubbing, or for finishing heads on nymphs and dry flies, I have found none better than clear nail polish, which in case you didn't know is merely a high-grade lacquer that happens also to be a good binding agent for various parts of a fishing fly.

413M	Palest gray (can be used as a neutral color)
162M	Creamish pink
176M	Light rosy pink
136M	Bright yellow
150M	Bright orange
165M	Reddish orange
583M	Light green
104M	Light olive
347M	Grass green
115M	Yellow

Like so many things in fly tying, an individual's taste in colors is personal, and insects found in different parts of the country may vary in shade and not completely coincide with the colors I have chosen. By all means use your own judgment.

LEAD WIRE

For additional weight on nymphs and other subaquatic artificials, lead wire can be purchased wound on spools or in a coil ready to use. The diameter of the wire should be selected carefully to suit the size of the fly. The most commonly used diameters are from .010 to .035, which is not to say that others are not useful at one time or another, but most dressings in this book do not call for any smaller or larger than those in this range. When dressing the larger stonefly nymphs I often use heavy monofilament to tie onto the sides of a hook shank when an especially wide body is needed.

FLOSS AND WOOL

Although none of my patterns calls for floss or wool to be used as a finishing material, it is often used to wind over an underbody on large nymphs to build it up before applying fur or latex. The floss can be either silk or nylon and comes on spools with single or four-strand lengths. I prefer the four-strand, which is quicker to use when building up a heavy body, and if need be, I cut a single strand from the same spool for smaller flies. A good crewel wool is all you need for underbodies and comes in many

FELT-TIP MARKING PENS

The use of waterproof marking pens in fly tying is nothing new. It is an easy, convenient method of achieving the two-toned effect so often needed when copying insects with a distinct color difference between the top and bottom. The mistake that many have made is to use dime-store markers that are not waterproof. Then the markings fade and wash away after the first trip in the water. After experimenting with various brands of pens, I have come to the conclusion that the Pantone markers are superior for our type of work and come in a full range of colors, and then some. Availability is an important factor when recommending a product, and marking pens are no exception. Pantone pens can be purchased in any reasonably well-stocked art supply store. While in the store, ask the clerk for a color chart for future reference.

For tinting work on artificials, including those in this book, I use the following colors:

Black M	Black
154M	Brown
464M	Brown
499M	Mahogany
438M	Dark brownish purple
404M	Gray

colors from your supplier or department store. Either single-strand or four-strand will do nicely. Choose your colors of floss and wool so they are similar to that of the underbody, or the translucency of fur or latex may give the finished fly a different shade than was intended.

TAILS FOR NYMPHS

Tail materials for nymphs are not hard to get; you probably already have most of the feathers in your material stock.

The goose-wing quill fibers for stoneflies are taken from the leading edge of the feather (short fibered side on a pointer), where they are usually a little firmer than on the other side of the quill stem. The reason for using white goose quills is to enable the tier to tint them with the same color marking pen as the rest of the fly.

The two feathers most widely used for tails on nymphs are wood duck flank feather and cock pheasant center tail. Pheasant feathers vary in shade from tan to brown and purplish brown. The fibers are quite strong and are far preferable to anything else for nymphs within their color range. Fibers from wood duck flank feathers are pale olive brown with fine brown markings and imitate well the tails on many of our common nymphs.

To best imitate the fanlike hairy tails on some swimming and burrowing nymphs there is nothing better and more realistic than the tips from mini-ostrich herl, the dun-gray color in particular. They are hard to get from your supplier, but often you can buy a feather duster in a household supply store made from just such feathers, which should give you a lifetime supply.

I can think of only one occasion where peacock herl is used for tails—on the *Isonychia* nymph. Tips from the metallic-green herl turn brown when underwater, and, if I am not mistaken, the entire nymph is often dressed from herl for that reason.

TAILS FOR DRY FLIES

Unlike traditional dry flies, which depend heavily on their tails to float in the proper manner, the tails on the flies in this book are of little consequence; at the most, they play a minor role in adding to the attractiveness of the fly. Perhaps in the case of the spinner they aid in stabilizing the fly and keeping the heavier end of the hook from submerging completely. Therefore, the best and stiffest hackle you've set aside for tails should be reserved for spinner imitations, and the less desirable should be used for tails that are set up at an angle so that they rarely come in contact with water. Aside from hackle fibers, it's possible to use wood duck flank feathers and moose or elk mane, materials that formerly would have been sneered at by most, at least for tailing of dry flies.

FEATHERS FOR ABDOMEN EXTENSIONS

I mentioned earlier that the materials list includes feathers rarely used in fly dressing. Those for extensions fall into that category. They do so simply because of the characteristics needed in feathers for such work. They must in most cases be body feathers or small spade hackles with a good webby portion that will make the fibers bulky enough when set in glue and compressed into the form of the mayfly abdomen. While I prefer small spade hackles where the fibers in the tip end are usually nice and stiff for imitating tails in the end of the body, I also use the yellowish-tan breast from cock pheasant, wood duck, teal, and mallard flank feathers in their natural colors or dyed to imitate a particular insect. For the smallest realistics where bulk is a major problem, I prefer a small hen neck hackle if the right color is available, or use the simplified extensions of trimmed and lacquered hackle explained in subsequent chapters.

WINGS FOR DRY FLIES

Our forefathers would probably turn over in their graves if they found out that anything as simple as deer body hair was being used for winging of dry flies, and yet it beats anything else I've ever tried. The fine-textured hair is best and causes less flare and bulk when fastened on the hook. When tied in, the butt ends are trimmed to form an underbody that, in combination with the fur, makes the flies all but unsinkable. However, care must be taken when selecting the deer hair so the sometimes heavily marked hair tips do not clash with the overall color scheme of the artificial; if necessary, they must even be dyed to resemble the color of the natural insect wings.

There is no doubt that wings are important for added effectiveness of an artificial fishing fly, and those trimmed to shape from thin, delicate body feathers of blue-dun rooster or hen in different shades very closely resemble the real thing. For the smallest flies I can think of, there is nothing I'd rather use than small neck feathers from a hen. These small feathers are usually wide and firm enough to trim well, and they have a curve in the stem that is almost prefect to produce the proper amount of wing separation when they are set together upright on the hook. There are, of course, many other usable feathers, but most are either not delicate enough or the stems are too heavy and curved. While the aforementioned are ideally suited for flies with wings of a blue-gray or pale-blue-dun color, there are insects for which they are definitely not suitable because the natural insects feature heavily marked wings of an entirely different shade. However, there are other feathers that lend themselves well to this work. Although not as desirable in quality, mallard, teal, and wood duck feathers have markings resembling the naturals, as do the small gray and brown partridge body hackles, all of which can be dyed if necessary. The most natural-looking of them all, however, is a feather I use for the March Brown. It is found on the back of a cock pheasant near the root of the tail. The markings and general color make for a very convincing set of wings.

WINGS FOR CADDIS DRY FLIES

The traditional method of winging the caddis adult was to use a wing quill segment dressed low-wing in a roof-like manner and then trimmed a bit in the end. It was a fragile arrangement; like other quill wings, it would split rather quickly and ruin the fly's appearance and performance. This has in later years been changed to a better, more durable wing structure of hair. The silhouette of a small bunch of deer body hair or the guard hairs from the very popular mink tail can't be beat. Mink tails are available from your supplier in a variety of colors specifically chosen with caddis dry flies in mind.

Fine-textured deer body hair with or without markings is readily available; most fly tiers have it in their material stock anyway.

WINGS FOR TERRESTRIALS

Wing arrangements on the terrestrial insects of value to the fly fisher are relatively simple, consisting in some cases of a combination under and over wing, a dressing method creating a better silhouette. The cricket and hopper imitations are good examples of such wing arrangements. It is best to use natural crow wing quill sections on the cricket, although suppliers may not have it and just give you dyed black mallard, which is acceptable if it is well dyed. The hopper uses a mottled-brown turkey-wing quill section of medium shade. When buying the wing feathers, it is best to get a matched pair even though only a segment from one feather is needed. There are probably other flies you can use the matched feathers for.

Deer body hair is used on both insects, either in its natural color or dyed black. The same black deer hair is used for dressing the black beetle, and when you see a piece of well-dyed material you shouldn't hesitate to grab it, as most dye jobs are poor and the surface will often be crisp and disintegrated.

Feathers for wings on the "Feather Beetle" are from the collar of a cock pheasant. The metallic-colored feathers around the neck—the "ring neck"—are not easy to get from a supplier. If you have a friend who hunts, ask him to bring a bird to you for a "harvest," or perhaps a complete skinning job.

WING CASES FOR NYMPHS AND CADDIS PUPAE

The latex and fur wing-case arrangements on mayfly and stonefly nymphs are discussed elsewhere in this chapter.

Wing cases for nymphs and pupae are made from quill segments. A good assortment should include turkey, mallard, teal, and two others which are not wing quills but tail feathers—the dark-brown mottled turkey tail for the hellgrammite and the short tail from a cock pheasant for the *Stenonema* nymphs. When a plain shade is called for, it can be taken from a hen wing or dyed mallard. As in many other instances, there are no set rules for the type of feathers used as long as they are similar to those called for in the dressing.

HACKLE

It was the scarcity of good hackle that led me to decide there was a future for flies that require no floating hackle; a couple of turns of "half-good" hackle will at least represent the insect legs and stabilize the fly while it floats in its fur body. This is by no means a new idea, merely an old method that has become popular lately. The reason, I suspect, is the same as mine— there is simply not enough good hackle to go around.

It is always best to buy whole necks rather than loose hackles that might be taken from different birds and are not uniform in color. Even though only one hackle is required for the mayfly duns, the caddis dry flies deserve two of the best "same-colored" hackles you can get.

The following is a listing of the rooster and hen necks, and whole rooster saddles, I most frequently use:

White These hackles will often have creamy shine on top; they are better than the pure white, which are generally of poor quality. White hackles are needed for dyeing to particular shades that are so often not obtainable.

Cream While the white hackles may have cream in them, it is usually pale; the color you need is somewhere between a white and a very pale ginger.

Light Ginger A pale-tan shade.

Dark Ginger A very light brown shade.

Natural Red These hackles have a color that is somewhere between brown and reddish-brown.

Coachman Brown These hackles from a saddle make good extensions for the *Isonychia* Realistic, etc. The shade is a sort of flat brown to mahogany.

Coch-y-Bondhu A dark-brown shade with black edges. I use this particular combination for extensions on the *Leptophlebia* realistics.

Furnace These hackles are brown to dark brown, with a black center stripe running down the middle. Sometimes you find hackles on a skin that are shiny ginger-colored with a black stripe. They are very effective for the parachute leg hackle; they produce darkened areas near the wing on top of the thorax, and yet the legs are very light.

Badger These are important to me and I use them frequently. Shades in these hackles vary from white to gold edges with a black center stripe. While the white-edged ones have their uses, I prefer the golden badger for the Green Drake and some of the Blue-Wing Olives. The rarest variations are those hackles with a bronze-colored edge, and needless to say, they are also very useful for many important dressings of the season.

Grizzly These have black and white bars and come from Plymouth Rock hens and roosters. The ones I prefer, though, are the variants with shades from ginger to golden ginger and brown all mixed in a combination on one hackle. They are, of course, strictly freaks and referred to as "Grizzly Multi-Variants." They are particularly effective for parachute hackle on March Browns and the Gray Foxes. If they are not available, the ordinary grizzly can be dyed any color.

Blue Dun Natural blue-dun necks are not only hard to get, but also hard to describe. Over the years I have had necks that ranged from almost completely black to very palest gray. Before you spend your hard-earned dollars on the natural necks, which, incidentally, are rarely of good quality, look into photo-dyed necks. They are nothing less than spectacular in every sense of the word. By photo-dying different shades—for example, a ginger—of natural necks, you are able to come up with a rusty dun, pale-blue dun, and many of the medium-to-dark shades so often used when dressing the Hendricksons, etc.

FUR

Most experienced fly tiers will agree that fur is the most important material used in the dressing of artificial flies. In fact, I have often stated that if I had to choose one material and discard all the rest, I would never hesitate to keep my fur. The question of which kind of fur is best is, of course, an entirely different story; each individual will usually select the kind that is best suited to the particular flies he is tying. Generally speaking, though, one can divide fur into two categories: the fine-textured mink, beaver, rabbit, opossum, and others which are mostly used for dry flies; and the rougher-textured underfur from such animals as the red and gray fox, woodchuck, and black and brown bear that are primarily used for nymphs and other subaquatic artificials. There are, of course, many others, of which a few will be explained later in the chapter.

The best way of obtaining a great many different-textured furs is to visit your local furrier and ask if he has any scraps or trimmings he wants to part with. Sometimes you will be doing him a favor by picking it off the floor, and sometimes he will charge you a few bucks, but it's worth it. Also, your material supplier has a long list of fur from which to choose; when looking through the various catalogues it seems as if anything

"furry" has a use in fly tying. However, as you progress in your fly-tying efforts and engage in more advanced work, you will become more selective and more carefully choose the type of fur that has the characteristics you need when dressing a specific insect imitation.

Using the exact fur I prescribe is not nearly as critical for the dry flies in this book as for the nymphs; the dries can be dressed with any of the fine-textured furs mentioned earlier, either in their natural shade or thoroughly dyed.

Fur Dubbing for Dry Flies, Duns, Spinners, and Caddisflies

While I advocate the use of natural shades, it is just not possible to get the olives, yellows, greens, and so forth in natural shades, and they must be dyed. Bleached fur is very good, and many bleached animal furs turn fine creamish or tan shades, that are used alone or blended with other colors. Mink fur is the best I can think of, and it is now available in a full range of natural and dyed colors.

Fur Dubbing for Nymphs

If you have jumped ahead in this book and looked at the tying instructions and materials lists for the various nymphs, you will have found that there is a considerable difference between my patterns and the traditional dressings of yesterday, both in the material used and in the method of tying. This is not to make things more difficult, but rather to help the fly dresser of today who seeks to achieve more realism in his artificials and who wishes to learn new and practical ways of doing it.

Many years ago, I used baby seal's fur for dubbing the abdomen, and I rarely mixed it with anything except an occasional touch of gray beaver to get a dirty shade, or with other colors for the dubbing used when dressing the smaller flies where pure seal would be too coarse. Now that seals are on the Endangered Species List, there is a need for a good substitute. Thanks to modern technology I was able to secure a type of material that apparently has all the characteristics of the real thing. It has an even better sheen, and the texture is such that it can easily be dubbed on your tying thread. But best of all, the translucency of this high-quality substitute is magnificent. When dubbed on the abdomen portion of a nymph it can be trimmed flat, and you can pick it out to imitate the gills that are present on most nymphs. Seal-Ex and SLF are now available from your supplier in sets of many different colors for mixing.

Fur for Legs, Thorax, and Wing Case
This is by far the most important and most difficult type of fur to select, and I can't emphasize strongly enough that you take your time in selecting and practicing the method of dubbing the legs, thorax, and wing case in one application. For this work the fur must be taken off the skin unblended, because the secret to success lies in using the guard hairs and underfur as it is cut from the skin, with the natural direction of both being undisturbed.

The two types that I like best for all my nymphs are, first, the belly, neck, leg, and mask of an Australian opossum; and second, the well-marked guard hair and fur from the back of a brown rabbit. If you are lucky enough to obtain a complete skin of an Australian opossum, you have covered your needs for mayfly nymphs. The brown rabbit with its longer back fur and well-marked guard hairs is primarily used for legs and thorax on caddis pupae and larger stonefly nymphs, but there is no set rule as long as either fur will produce the desired result. Choosing the proper length of fur is the important thing, and while brown rabbit is not hard to get (some surplus stores around the country sell whole skins for a couple of dollars), the opossum may have to be purchased in small pieces from which you can select what you need. The alternatives are mink and hare's mask, and I am sure there are others just as useful.

Cutting the Fur Layer
I mentioned earlier that the length of the fur is important, and I would like to repeat this. Legs on the nymphs are usually sized to be half a body length (with perhaps the exception of the large

Hexagenia and *Ephemera,* which are about one-third a body length). A good guideline to remember about the length is to make them as long as two hook gaps. Personally, I prefer the legs to be too short rather than too long, but that is strictly an individual preference. A piece of back fur from a brown rabbit or a piece of opossum can be used for the thorax/leg construction. The rule to follow when selecting the fur is quite simple—the smaller the fly the softer the fur. Opossum is generally used for flies from size 12 and down, while rabbit is used for anything larger than that. The rabbit back fur may feel soft to you, but when cut from the skin and trimmed to length, the guard hairs are actually very stiff. Of course, all fur and guard hair is not of the same length all over an animal and it is always a good practice to keep pieces of skin from different parts of the pelt handy.

When a thin fur layer has been cut from the edge of a piece of skin it will nearly always have to be trimmed to length. This is done by holding the fur by the tips and trimming the butt portion.

LATEX
Until Raleigh Boaze, Jr., discovered the use of latex as the ultimate answer to the fly-tier's need for a super body material, I thought that everything that could possibly be wound, spun, or glued on a hook had been tried. Raleigh started a brand new chapter in American fly tying, and I predict that the future will continue to bring many new artificials into popularity.

Latex is available from your supplier in 5 × 5-inch sheets that can be cut in strips of any width. Do not be misled into thinking that very thin latex can be used. The thickness best suited for flies is designated by the manufacturer as Heavy, .0112 to .0115. To cut it one can use a paper cutter or simply a sharp razor blade or X-Acto knife. Either way I find it best to sandwich the latex between two pieces of cardboard or it is difficult to control. The width of the strips needed for a particular nymph is indicated in its pattern. Latex can be dyed as you would dye fur and feathers, and it is easily tinted with waterproof marking pens.

OTHER MATERIALS

Larvae Lace
Micro-thin rubber-like rubbing material used for whole nymph bodies and for ribbing on stonefly nymphs, available in many different colors.

Bucktail
Dyed in different colors, these tails are used for wings on large streamers and for legs on the Hammerhead.

Arctic Fox Tail
A wonderful soft hair used in wings on many baitfish imitations, available in many different colors.

Silver Fox Tail
Very much like Arctic fox, but longer in the fiber. Used in wings on larger baitfish imitations.

Icelandic Hair
A very long, soft hair for use in the big streamers. Can be as long as 7 inches and is available in many colors.

Flashabou
A thin Mylar tinsel that can be mixed in with wings on streamers to create a flash. It comes in many different colors. Pearl, gold, and silver are the ones I use the most for the flies in this book.

Opposite: *Playing with hair, feather, and hooks at the vise at home has resulted in a beautiful cutthroat trout.*

Chapter 3
Mayfly Nymphs

TYPES OF NATURAL MAYFLY NYMPHS

The nymphal forms of our mayflies are very important to the angler who expects to achieve some degree of success, and they constitute a considerable portion of a fish's diet. They are found in most Eastern and Western streams capable of generating sufficient oxygen for them to live. Unlike adult mayflies, which are almost identical in appearance in all species, the nymphs are different. They can be divided into four groups of particular interest to the angler, each with some structural characteristics of its own, and each with an individual choice of habitat.

Conventional nymph patterns used in the past almost without exception used only color and size as their principal identification features, and this may have limited their effectiveness as representatives for specific nymphs. The discovery of new materials and techniques and the high development of fly-tying skill in America have now made it possible to treat each nymphal form individually, with special attention to the main features that characterize the particular insect it was made to imitate.

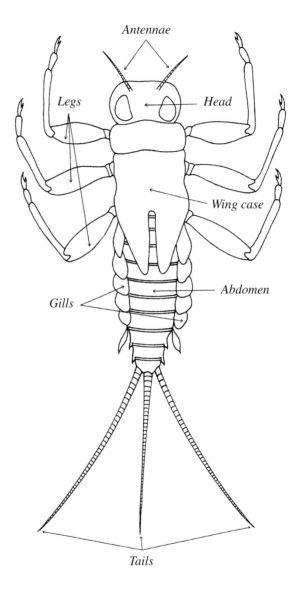

Anatomy of a mayfly nymph

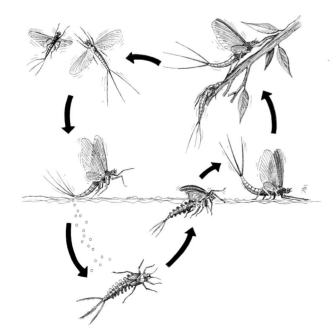

Left: *Lifecycle of the mayfly*

Clinging Species

The nymphs of this group are very flat and rather broad anteriorly, with flat, robust-looking legs. They can be found clinging to the underside of rocks and other objects where they are well hidden from predators. They inhabit fast water with plenty of oxygen, but before hatching they move to shallow areas where they can easily be collected if specimens are needed as models. The ones best known are those of the *Stenonema* and *Iron* genera.

Burrowing Species

This type of nymph is the most unusual and interesting one. Like a mole, it plows its way through the muddy bottom and debris. The structure of the burrowing nymph makes it easy to recognize. It is rather long, slender, and oval in cross section, which flattened legs and a large tusk-like projection on either side of the abdomen; on artificial flies these projections are referred to as gills. The *Ephemera* and the large *Hexagenia* nymphs belong to the burrowing group.

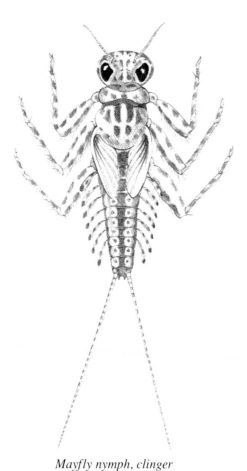

Mayfly nymph, clinger

Mayfly nymph, burrower

Sprawling Species

Nymphs belonging to the sprawling group move around slowly in all types of water, where they inhabit vegetation, gravel, and debris. The legs are thin and rather feeble in comparison with the clingers, and their bodies are round or oval in cross section, depending on the species. Specimens can be collected in a seine by shaking vegetation or moving debris on the stream bottom. Genera include *Ephemerella, Leptophlebia,* and *Caenis.*

Climber Species

These are free-ranging nymphs found in fast water where they dart, run, or swim around in the vegetation like minnows. They are very slender and streamlined with feeble legs like the sprawlers. The body is oval and the tails are usually heavily fringed. They can be collected in the same manner as the sprawlers.

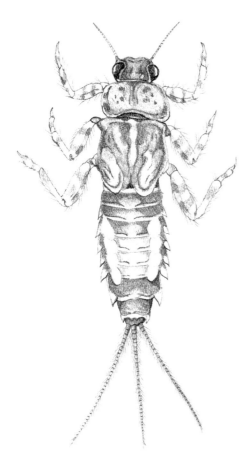

Mayfly nymph, sprawler

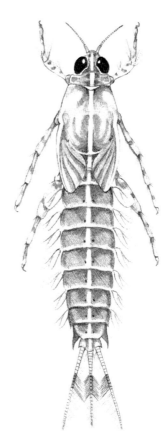

Mayfly nymph, climber

The group to which a particular nymph belongs will be indicated with each dressing pattern in this chapter. In most cases the structural differences between one nymph and another depend mostly on the amount of material used and how it is trimmed or picked out before or after being applied on the hook. As an example, if a nymph is very flat with long gills, the fur for the abdomen should be teased up before it is wound on the hook, and the body should be trimmed more on the top and bottom than one with an oval shape. If a nymph has medium to short gills, the fur need not be teased and the trimming will usually bring out sufficient fibers to imitate gills. What really is achieved with this method of dressing is a translucency and silhouette not possible with any other method that I know of.

DRESSING THE MAYFLY NYMPH, STEP BY STEP

I have chosen the *Stenonema* nymph as a model for the dressing instructions because of its large size and claim to fame as a good fish-getter. The nymphs belong to a group of several clingers of importance to the angler. Their flattish appearance can be well imitated by using the loop method to spin the dubbing. There are three related species of the *Stenonema* genus that are almost identical and with which the angler should be familiar: *S. vicarium* (March Brown), the largest of the three: *S. fuscum* (Gray Fox,) the middle-sized representative; and *S. canadense* (Light Cahill), the smallest of the group. Since they are all so well known, none should go unmentioned, but for all practical purposes, the only difference between the three, at least as far as angling is concerned, is the size.

The Stenonema Nymph

Body Length	9 to 16mm
Common Names	March Brown, Gray Fox, Light Cahill
Genus	*Stenonema*
Species	*vicarium, fuscum, canadense*

Availability   These nymphs are quite common in Eastern and Midwestern streams capable of generating sufficient oxygen. When they are ready to hatch (hatching usually starts in late May and lasts through mid-June, depending on temperature and locale), the nymphs migrate to shallow areas and during such times are often deadly and irresistible to the fish.

Very often the adults have some difficulty in escaping the nymphal skin, or for other reasons are unable to leave the water surface immediately and find themselves floating and struggling for a long time, a circumstance which permits the trout to feed on them in a leisurely manner without expending too much energy. For this reason an emerger-type artificial is often needed to get the full benefit of a hatch. The best known is the Hare's Ear, for which the dressing is listed in the section with additional nymph dressings. The other is the nymph dressing covered in the tying instructions, with one notable difference. The wing-case fur is left long, untrimmed, and unlacquered, thus giving the appearance of a partly emerged dun, or a struggling one unable to take off. The artificial should not be weighted, but instead must be given some dry-fly flotant, usually a silicone type like Gehrke's Gink, which can be smeared lightly on the underside.

Hook	Mustad 38941, size 10 to 12 and Mustad 3906B, size 12 to 16
Thread	Brown, prewaxed 6/0
Tails	Three brown fibers from cock pheasant center tail, one hook length long
Abdomen	Pale-amber Seal-Ex dubbing tinted brown on top
Gills	Medium, roughed-up dubbing
Thorax and Legs	Bleached opossum fur with guard hairs, or rabbit dyed tannish-amber; material applied fairly heavy
Wing Case	Trimmed thorax fur lacquered, or segment from short pheasant tail, underside up, or latex dyed dark brown and trimmed
Head	Brown tying thread
Dubbing Formula	1 part reddish-brown, 2 parts cream, mixed
Tinting	Since this nymph is lighter underneath than it is on top, the back is tinted lightly with brown Pantone 154M. This is not a solid tint and the amber should show on the back for the best effect. If a *fur* wing case is used, it should be tinted with the same color brown as the back of the abdomen. When dyed brown latex is used, the tip of the trimmed wing case is tinted lightly with a gray Pantone 404M to produce a blackish effect like the wing-case tips of the natural.

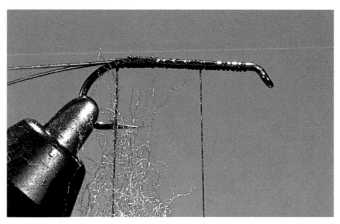

1. Tie in the tail fibers securely on the shank above a point midway between the hook point and the barb. I have never found that it makes any difference whether the fibers are splayed as the natural at rest or not. If additional weight is needed, it should be applied now. This can best be done by tying in a lead strip on one side of the hook shank and covering it with tying thread so that the flatness of the body can be maintained. Now form a spinning loop where the tails are tied in and insert a generous amount of dubbing.

2. Spin a ropelike dubbing that is fairly tight, well tapered, and heavy.

4. Apply some clear cement on the hook shank and wind the dubbing on the shank with close turns, stroking back the loosened fibers in the process and thus creating a fuzzy-looking body portion. Tie off about one-third hook length from the eye and make a couple of half-hitches.

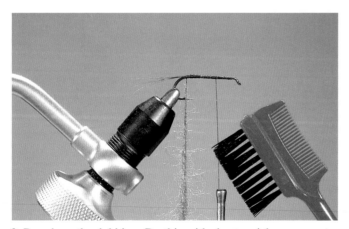

3. Rough up the dubbing. Do this with short, quick movements all the way around and for the full length of the dubbing. Care should be taken to only rough up the dubbing, not rip off the fibers as they will aid in achieving the flatness in the body and also represent the medium-sized gills on the sides of the abdomen.

5. Trim the body on top and bottom. Cut the fuzzy dubbing, and dig a little way into the solid stuff without cutting the dubbing thread. Use short, quick clipping motions of the scissor points held horizontally along the body. Trim it the full body length. Trim the sides lightly to remove long, stray fibers, but leave the side dubbing long enough to represent the gills.

6. The finished abdomen portion. Note that the body for this particular nymph is rather broad anteriorly, like most clingers, and as all the bodies for this type of nymph, it is segmented and highly translucent. Now form a spinning loop directly in front of the abdomen.

8. Insert the fur into the loop. Note the proportional placement. It is well spread out, and by using the loop thread as a guideline, you will see that the fur bunch is much longer on one side of the loop than on the other. The longer side has the fur and guard hairs that will become the legs, and the short side becomes the thorax and wing case (if a fur wing case is desired).

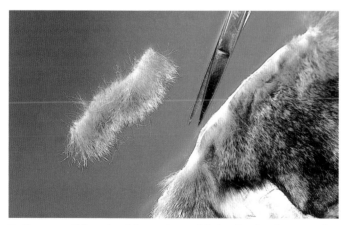

7. Cut a small bunch of fur and guard hairs for the thorax and legs. The whole bunch should be as long as half a body length. Do not disturb the natural direction of the fibers as they are to be used unmixed as they come off of the skin.

9. Spin a fur chenille.

10. Hold it up above the hook and moisten it a little before stroking all the fur and guard hairs back so it appears to be coming out from one side of the loop only.

12. Trim the fur and guard hair on top of the thorax, leaving it long enough to form an average-size wing case. Do not trim away the sides and bottom, as this material represents the legs.

11. Apply a little clear cement on the hook shank, then wind the fur on the thorax portion in front of the abdomen. Tie off in front, cut the surplus, and form a small head.

13. Brush or comb the fur a little so that the fibers are parallel with the body, then brush on a coat of clear nail polish. Press it flat a little with your fingers and trim the rear corners.

14. When it is dry, tint the wing case and top of the abdomen with a brown Pantone 154M and the nymph is finished. If you wish, you can trim along the center under the thorax, leaving enough on each side to represent the legs.

15. The finished Stenonema Nymph.

OTHER WING-CASE FORMS
The Latex Wing Case
While I prefer fur and quill-section wing cases on my nymphs, there are some who might find it simpler just to trim all the fur on top of the thorax and tie in a small trimmed section of latex for a wing case. This can be done in the following manner:

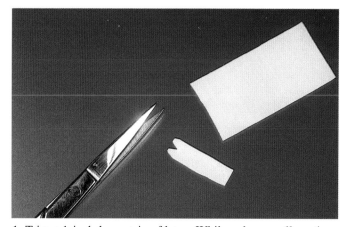

1. Trim a 1-inch-long strip of latex. While only a small portion of the length is used, it must be that long so that you can hold it while it is being tied in. The width is a little more than a body width of the nymph being dressed.

2. Lay the strip on top and tie it on in front. The latex must be held tightly when being secured or it will not stay on top. Now cut the surplus in front and leave the end exposed to imitate the head, or trim clean and wind the tying thread over it. The length of the wing case is usually a little shorter than half a body length; any deviation from this measurement will be indicated in the individual patterns.

The Quill Wing Case

In line with tradition, artificial nymphs are usually dressed with a wing case consisting of a quill section of the proper color tied in in front of the abdomen and folded forward over the thorax and tied down in front. This can also be done on the all-fur nymphs in the following manner:

3. When the latex wing case is first tied in, it may not lie down absolutely flat. If this is the case, tint it with a Pantone of the same color as the latex and it will automatically fall into place. When the Pantone dries, the latex may rise up a little, in which case apply a little cement on top of the thorax and underside of the wing case.

1. When the abdomen is finished and before the spinning loop for the leg and thorax fur is made, tie in a quill section of the material specified for the wing case in the pattern. The width of the section should be slightly more than that of the body, and the first tie-in windings must hold the quill section tightly against the front of the abdomen.

Cut the surplus short of the eye and wind some thread over the ends to bind them down on the shank. Take the thread to the extreme front of the abdomen and form a spinning loop.

2. Then, divide the fur on top down the middle and press it down to each side of the thorax. Now fold the quill section forward over the thorax and tie off in front. Cut the surplus quill before winding the head and applying some clear cement.

Selected Nymph and Important Emerger and Wet-Fly Dressings

Important note: Also, although I find SLF and Seal-Ex to be the best material for nymph bodies, any of the coarser furs like the foxes or the bear and woodchuck may be used if you wish, but they somehow lack the translucency of SLF and Seal-Ex. All the nymphs included below, with one exception, can be dressed with either of three wing-case forms.

1. Trimmed, lacquered, and tinted thorax fur.

2. Trimmed and tinted latex.

3. Wing quill section of the color indicated for the wing case.

The *Ephoron* nymph is the exception; the only material used for the case is deer hair. The thorax and leg fur method of dressing may seem awkward in the beginning (see Chapter 2 for fur types), but you will soon get the hang of it, and the amount of time spent learning pays dividends on the stream in the form of *fish*.

The most frustrating experience when fishing a nymph is inability to control the sink rate. I suggest that the nymph be dressed both weighted and unweighted in anticipation of fishing different types of water. The weight, in the form of thin lead wire, may be tied on the sides of the shank for the flat clinger-type nymphs, or simply wound like thread around the hook shank. I rarely use anything heavier than .010 lead wire, which is thin enough not to ruin the appearance of the nymph.

Adoptiva Nymph (crawler)

Body Length	6 to 8mm
Common Names	Blue Quill, Blue Dun, Little Blue Mayfly
Genus	*Paraleptophlebia*
Species	*adoptiva*
Availability	Anglers in the East and Midwest who have

enough courage to travel to their favorite stream in the sometime chilly weather of mid-April will probably find the Little Blue Quill on the water, and it usually remains there through May. The little *adoptiva* nymph is very effective shortly after noon, before hatching, when fished at almost any depth; a greased one may be fished successfully right in the surface film.

Hook	Mustad 3906B, size 16 to 18
Thread	Brown, prewaxed 6/0
Tails	Three wood duck fibers, one-half body length
Abdomen	Yellow-brown Seal-Ex dubbing or SLF
Gills	Picked out long
Thorax and Legs	Medium-brown guard hairs with fur
Wing Case	Dark grayish-brown
Head	Brown tying thread
Dubbing Formula	3 parts medium brown, 1 1/2 parts yellow
Tinting	Fur or latex wing case tinted dark gray with Pantone 404M

Baetis Nymph (swimmer)

Body Length	5 to 10mm
Common Name	Blue-Winged Olive
Genus	*Baetis*
Species	Various
Availability	*Baetis* are among the most important

insects for the trout angler and are present and active on streams throughout the country from April through September, *Baetis vagans*, a size 16 to 18 medium olive-brown nymph, is particularly useful for those who fish the famous limestone streams of Pennsylvania.

Hook	Mustad 94840, size 20 or Mustad 3906B, size 16 to 18
Thread	Olive, prewaxed 6/0
Tails	Three wood duck fibers, half a body length
Abdomen	SLF, Seal-Ex, or fur: 1. Dark brown 2. Medium olive-brown 3. Dark olive 4. Medium brown
Gills	Fibers appearing on sides after trimming abdomen are sufficient
Thorax and Legs	Grayish-brown guard hairs with fur; on the smallest nymphs a sparse amount of fur is applied and the legs picked out
Wing Case	Dark grayish brown
Head	Olive tying thread
Dubbing Formula	Dubbing #2: 1 part medium brown and 1 part medium olive
Tinting	Fur on latex wing case tinted with gray Pantone 404M

Blue-Winged Olive Nymph (sprawler)

Body Length	7 to 9mm
Common Names	Blue-Wing Olive, Small Dun Variant, Little Olive Cut-Wing
Genus	*Ephemerella*
Species	*attenuata*

Availability   This is another of the many super flies in the East, and although the species *E. attenuata* is particularly active prior to hatching, usually in late May and continuing through the better part of June, it lends itself well as a representative for other similar flies found throughout the country and can be dressed in any size. *E. attenuata* is one species that hatches under water like *Epeorus pleuralis* (Quill Gordon), and a wet fly, for which I also give the dressing, often works better than the nymph.

Hook	Mustad 3906B, size 14 to 16
Thread	Black, prewaxed 6/0
Tails	Three wood duck flank feather fibers, two-thirds body length
Abdomen	Dark-brownish-olive SLF or Seal-Ex dubbing
Gills	Picked out lightly
Thorax and Legs	Medium-olive-brown guard hairs with fur
Wing Case	Black
Head	Black tying thread
Dubbing Formula	2 parts medium brown, 2 parts light olive, and 1 part black
Tinting	Fur wing case tinted dark brown with Pantone 154M; latex wing case first tinted with brown Pantone 154M, then touched up with a little gray Pantone 404M

Blue-Winged Olive (wet fly)

Hook	Mustad 3906B, size 14 to 16
Thread	Olive, prewaxed 6/0
Tails	Light-blue-dun hackle fibers
Body	Yellowish-olive fur dubbing
Hackle	Medium-blue-dun hen hackle, soft
Wings	Blue-gray duck-wing quill sections, tied downwing
Head	Olive tying thread
Dubbing Formula	1 part yellow and 1 part olive fur

Caenis Nymph (sprawler)

Body Length	4 to 5mm
Common Names	Angler's Curse, Tiny White-Winged Dun
Genus	*Tricorythodes*
Species	Various

Availability   Found throughout the country. Active period from June through September, depending on locale.

Hook	Mustad 3906, size 18
Thread	Olive, prewaxed 6/0
Tails	Three brown fibers from cock pheasant center tail, half a body length
Abdomen	Grayish-brown fur dubbing
Thorax and Legs	Dark-grayish-brown fur with short guard hairs
Wing Case	Trimmed thorax fur, lacquered and tinted
Head	Olive tying thread
Dubbing Formula	2 parts medium-brown fur and 1 part medium-gray fur
Tinting	Fur wing case tinted lightly with gray Pantone 404M

Epeorus Nymph (clinger)

Body Length	11 to 15mm
Common Names	Gordon Quill, Quill Gordon, Iron Dun
Genus	*Epeorus*
Species	*pleuralis, fraudator*
Availability	For many years this fly has been among

the best-known in America, and still is for that matter. It is the one fly the angler thinks of at the outset of each new season. Nymphs are active just before a hatch; hatching usually occurs from mid-April through mid-May and starts shortly after noon. Since the fly hatches underwater, it is more effective to use a Quill Gordon wet fly during a hatch, and so I have included the wet-fly dressing below. However, I also use an emerger type of artificial, which is the *Epeorus* nymph with the wing-case fur left long and untrimmed. This version should be treated to float with a silicone such as Gehrke's Gink and fished in the surface film. Unlike the nymph-type artificial, the emerger is unweighted, thus enabling you to fish it right in the surface film.

Hook	Mustad 38941 3X Long, size 12 to 14 or Mustad 3906B, size 8 to 10
Thread	Olive, prewaxed 6/0
Tails	Two brown fibers from cock pheasant tail, one body length
Abdomen	Medium-brown SLF or Seal-Ex dubbing with a touch of olive
Gills	Picked out, heavy
Thorax and Legs	Medium-brown guard hairs with fur
Wing Case	Medium brown
Head	Olive tying thread
Dubbing Formula	10 parts medium brown and 1 part medium olive
Tinting	Fur and latex wing case should be tinted with brown Pantone 154M; latex wingtips are touched lightly with gray Pantone 404M

Quill Gordon (wet fly)

Hook	Mustad 3906B, size 12 to 14
Thread	Black, prewaxed 6/0
Tails	Rusty-blue-dun hackle fibers
Body	Stripped peacock quill
Hackle	Rusty-blue-dun hen hackle, soft
Wings	Wood duck flank feather, tied downwing
Head	Black tying thread

Ephemera Nymph (burrower)

Body Length	15 to 28mm
Common Names	Green Drake, Multi-Variant
Genus	*Ephemera*
Species	*guttulata*
Availability	This large, beautiful mayfly has undoubtedly

stirred up enough action and excitement to deserve a whole chapter of its own. The nymph pattern is a good representative for several flies of the same genus when dressed in different sizes. Although it has often been said that the nymph of a Green Drake is not effective, I have had extremely good luck with a heavily weighted nymph size 4 3X Long. Cast it upstream, let it sink deep and come down drag-free until it is almost in front of you, then quickly raise it to the surface. That is when the trout hits it.

Hook	Mustad 38941 3X Long, size 4 to 10
Thread	Brown, prewaxed 6/0
Tails	Three light-tannish-gray mini-ostrich herl tips, one-third body length
Abdomen	Light-amber SLF or Seal-Ex dubbing with brown back markings
Gills	Abdomen fur teased up before it is wound; pick out gills further after body is trimmed for tusklike heavy gills; may be tinted gray
Thorax and Legs	Creamish-amber guard hairs with fur
Wing Case	Medium brown
Head	Brown tying thread
Dubbing Formula	3 parts cream, 2 parts yellow, and 1 part reddish-brown
Tinting	Fur or latex wing case is tinted brown with Pantone 154M; the tips on the latex case are touched lightly with gray Pantone 404M; back markings are made with Pantone 154M; gills tinted with gray Pantone 404M

Ephemerella Nymph (crawler)

Body Length	9 to 12mm
Common Names	Hendrickson, Red Quill, Beaverkill
Genus	*Ephemerella*
Species	*subvaria, invaria, rotunda*
Availability	This is one of the best-known members

of the American fly hatches, at least in the East and Midwest, with some related species found in Western waters. The nymphs are most active and vulnerable to trout from the end of April through the beginning of June before hatching. I have made it one of my standard patterns for nymph fishing all year, both weighted and unweighted.

Hook	Mustad 3906B, size 10 to 12
Thread	Brown, prewaxed 6/0
Tails	Three light-brown fibers from cock pheasant center tail, one-half body length
Abdomen	Reddish-amber SLF or Seal-Ex dubbing, touch-tinted on the back
Gills	Picked out, medium
Thorax and Legs	Well-marked brown guard hairs with fur
Wing Case	Dark brown
Head	Brown tying thread
Dubbing Formula	2 parts cream, 1 part reddish brown, and 1 part yellow
Tinting	Fur or latex wing case is tinted dark brown with Pantone 154M; in addition, the tips on the trimmed latex case are touched lightly with gray Pantone 404M; the back of the abdomen is dabbed lightly with brown Pantone 154M, leaving the center one-third an untouched reddish-amber color; if you wish, the back can be left as is, without tint

Ephoron Nymph (burrower)

Body Length	11 to 13mm
Common Names	White Fly, White Miller
Genus	*Ephoron*
Species	Representative
Availability	These white flies are found in some Eastern

and Midwestern streams, and I have experienced blizzardlike hatches at twilight during the last two weeks of July on the Potomac River in western Maryland and in late August and September on the Yellow Breeches in Pennsylvania. The nymphs are active from late afternoon before a hatch, and they are fished as an emerger in most cases.

Hook	Mustad 38941 3X Long, size 12 to 14
Thread	Gray, prewaxed 6/0
Tails	Three grayish-white wing quill fibers, one-third body length
Abdomen	Dirty-white SLF or Seal-Ex and fur dubbing
Gills	Picked out, heavy
Thorax and Legs	Grayish-white fur with guard hairs
Wing Case	Medium-gray deer body hair over thorax, lacquered
Head	Gray tying thread
Dubbing Formula	White dubbing with gray fur added to produce a dirty-white color
Tinting	If natural deer body hair is used for the wing case, it should be tinted medium gray with Pantone 404M

Note: A small piece of orange silk floss is often added in front of the thorax as a beard before the head is wound. It should not be more than $1/16$-inch long. According to anglers on the Yellow Breeches, it makes the nymph more effective. The reason for having a deer-hair wing is to fish the nymph in the surface film with the front in the film and the abdomen riding downward at an angle. The front is often dressed with silicone flotant to achieve this.

Hexagenia Nymph (burrower)

Body Length	16 to 30mm
Common Names	Michigan Caddis, Fish Fly
Genus	*Hexagenia*
Species	Various
Availability	While flies of the *Hexagenia* genus are

found in both Eastern and Midwestern waters, they are best known for their appearance on Michigan streams from mid-June through the better part of August, depending on the area being fished. I use weighted versions of the *Hexagenia* nymph all year round, and the fish are always looking for a good-size meal, even early in the season.

Hook	Mustad 38941 3X Long, size 4
Thread	Brown, prewaxed 6/0
Tails	Three light-tannish-gray mini-ostrich herl tips, one-third body length
Abdomen	Amber SLF or Seal-Ex dubbing mixed with gray fur; purple-brown back markings at each abdomen segment
Gills	Abdomen fur teased up before being wound; after trimming top and bottom, pick out the gills further for tusk-like heavy gills; may be tinted
Thorax and Legs	Tan guard hairs with fur
Wing Case	Purplish-brown, one-third body length
Head	Brown tying thread
Dubbing Formula	1 part reddish brown, 2 parts yellow, 3 parts cream with medium-gray fur added to get a dirty or grayish amber
Tinting	Fur or latex wing case tinted purplish brown with Pantone 438M; back markings and light tinting of the gills are done with the same color marker

Isonychia Nymph (climber)

Body Length	16 to 20mm
Common Names	Dun Variant, White Gloved Howdy, Leadwing Coachman
Genus	*Isonychia*
Species	*bicolor, sadleri*

Availability Evening hatches of the slim, fast-swimming *Isonychia* nymphs take place on Eastern and Midwestern streams from late May through August. Aside from the stoneflies, this is the only nymph that I know of that crawls onto stones and debris out of the water to hatch. The exoskeletons are found along the rocky streamside and can be used for models, although such specimens are very fragile and should be handled with care. The best thing to do is to take a closeup photograph for your file. I usually weight these nymphs and find that they work better when applying a swimming action. As is the case with several other nymphs included in my list of important dressings, there is a related wet-fly pattern worthy of note. Who can forget the Leadwing Coachman with the sparkling peacock herl and slate-gray wings for an evening of good fishing? I have included the dressing below the nymph pattern for those who feel as I do that it's a "darn good fly."

Hook	Mustad 38941 3X Long or Partridge Swimming Nymph K6ST, size 8 to 10
Thread	Brown, prewaxed 6/0
Tails	Three peacock herl tips, one-third body length
Abdomen	Dark-purple-brown Seal-Ex dubbing with thin white medium stripe of goose-quill fiber or light moose-mane fiber tied down over abdomen and wing case (stripe optional)
Gills	Picked out, medium long
Thorax and Legs	Short well-marked grayish guard hairs and fur from hare's or opossum's mask
Wing Case	Dark grayish brown (wing case is rather pronounced and only one-third body length)
Head	Brown tying thread
Dubbing Formula	4 parts medium brown, 2 parts black, 1 part magenta, and 1 part reddish brown
Tinting	Fur or latex wing case is tinted with dark-brown Pantone 154M; in addition, the latex is also given a light touch of gray Pantone 404M to produce the dark-grayish-brown shade

Note: If you wish to dress the nymph with the white medium stripe on top, it is done in the following manner. When the tails have been tied in, tie in a 6-inch length of purple-colored tying thread, together with a white fiber from a goose wing quill or a light moose-mane fiber. The two materials should sit on top of the shank. Proceed to finish the abdomen portion, then lay the fiber over the top in the middle and use the purple thread to secure it. Tie it off in front of the abdomen. Do not cut the surplus fiber. When the thorax, leg portion, and wing case are finished, including tinting, the remainder is laid forward over the wing case and tied down in front before the head is wound, thus making the white stripe run the full length of the nymph. This is done only on the *bicolor* species; on *sadleri* the stripe is of little consequence.

Leadwing Coachman (wet fly)

Hook	Mustad 3906B, size 8 to 10
Thread	Black, prewaxed 6/0
Tail	None; instead, a small flat gold tinsel tag
Body	Peacock herl, fairly thick
Hackle	Reddish-brown hen hackle
Wings	Lead-colored starling wing quill sections
Head	Black tying thread

Leptophlebia Nymph (sprawler)

Body Length	10 to 12mm
Common Names	Black Quill, Whirling Dun, Cut-Wing Leptophlebia
Genus	*Leptophlebia*
Species	*cupida*
Availability	This dark-brown nymph is active all

through the day from late April through early June. Eastern anglers have used these dark nymphs for many years as an "all-purpose" nymph when dark flies abound, but since there are several related species found in Western waters, it is certainly not restricted to Eastern anglers.

Hook	Mustad 38941, 3X Long, size 12 to 14 or Mustad 3906B, size 8 to 10
Thread	Brown, prewaxed 6/0
Tails	Three medium-brown fibers from cock pheasant center tail, one body length
Abdomen	Dark-brown SLF or Seal-Ex dubbing with a touch of olive
Gills	Picked out, heavy
Thorax and Legs	Brown guard hairs with fur
Wing Case	Dark brown
Head	Brown tying thread
Dubbing Formula	5 parts dark-brown Seal-Ex and 1 part medium-olive fur
Tinting	Fur or latex wing case tinted brown with Pantone 154; wingtips on the latex touched lightly with gray Pantone 404M

Potamanthus Nymph (crawler)

Body Length	15mm
Common Names	Golden Drake, Cream Variant, Potamanthus Cut-Wing
Genus	*Potamanthus*
Species	*distinctus*
Availability	This nymph is active in Eastern and

Midwestern streams in the evening hours from mid-June to past mid-August, but can be used whenever a yellow-brown nymph of its size is needed.

Hook	Mustad 38941 3X Long, size 10
Thread	Brown, prewaxed 6/0
Tails	Three light-brown fibers from cock pheasant center tail, one-third body length
Abdomen	Yellow-brown SLF or Seal-Ex dubbing, reddish-brown back markings
Gills	Picked out, very long
Thorax and Legs	Yellow-brown guard hairs and fur
Wing Case	Reddish brown, one-third body length
Head	Brown tying thread
Dubbing Formula	3 parts medium brown and 1 1/2 parts yellow
Tinting	Fur or latex wing case tinted brown with Pantone 154M; tips on the latex case are touched slightly with gray Pantone 404M; back markings are applied with the same Pantone as used for tinting the wing case

Stenonema Nymph (clinger)

The dressing pattern and other related information pertaining to this important fly were covered earlier in this chapter and need not be repeated. However, I should like to include an old wet fly of traditional vintage which has undoubtedly undergone some changes since it was devised: the Gold-Ribbed Hare's Ear. Its classification could easily be that of an "all-purpose" wet fly that, dressed in different sizes, can be fished all year round with good success.

Gold-Ribbed Hare's Ear (wet fly)

Hook	Mustad 3906B, size 12 to 16 or Mustad 39041 3X Long, size 10 to 12
Thread	Black, prewaxed 6/0
Tails	Ginger hen hackle fibers
Body	Brownish-gray hare's mask or SLF dressed tapered but rough, ribbed with narrow gold tinsel
Hackle	A soft grouse or brown partridge body hackle; or picked-out fur and guard hairs from the body (on smaller sizes or if grouse or partridge is not available in the required sizes, the fibers can be tied in as a beard, with a smaller bunch tied in on top and sides to complete the "collar")
Wing	Brown mottled turkey-wing quill sections, tied downwing

Sulphur Nymph (sprawler)

Body Length	7 to 9mm
Common Names	Little Marryatt, Pale Evening Dun
Genus	*Ephemerella*
Species	*dorothea*
Availability	This fly is well known to Eastern and

Western anglers and has enjoyed a generous amount of publicity over the years. The fish seem to be more fond of the emerger type of artificial, and at times trout will completely ignore the freshly hatched dun and feed on the emerging nymph on the surface. The Little Marryatt wet fly, for which I have also included the dressing, or the Sulphur Nymph, with the wing-case fur left long and unlacquered, both work well. The emerger nymph version must be treated with some silicone grease such as Gehrke's Gink.

Hook	Mustad 3906B, size 14 to 16
Thread	Brown, prewaxed 6/0
Tails	Three pale-tan fibers from cock pheasant center tail or wood duck flank fibers, one-half body length
Abdomen	Yellowish-brown SLF or Seal-Ex dubbing
Gills	Picked out, lightly
Thorax and Legs	Tan guard hairs with fur
Wing Case	Brown (if made with feather case, use brown mottled turkey-wing quill section)
Head	Brown tying thread
Dubbing Formula	1 part reddish brown, 1 part yellow, and 3 parts cream
Tinting	Fur or latex wing case tinted with brown Pantone 154M; wingtips on the latex touched lightly with gray Pantone 404M

Emerger: *The wing case guard hair and underfur should not be trimmed or lacquered; when left long it imitates a partially emerged dun or struggling nymph unable to take off from the surface. This type of fly should not be weighted, but rather sprayed or greased with Gehrke's Gink or other flotant.*

From Left: Hexagenia *nymph,* Isonychia *nymph, and mayfly nymph.*

Opposite: *The author fishes a small mountain stream.*

Chapter 4
Mayfly Duns and Spinners

The delicate insects of the mayfly order, the Ephemeroptera, do not distinguish themselves by being particularly colorful and will appear to the naked eye in rather subdued shades ranging from dark mahogany to pale pastels in olive green and pink. Their graceful anatomy, however, has made them the primary target for fly tiers with enough ambition and desire to create artificials that in appearance are extremely realistic-looking. Unfortunately, the most beautiful mayfly masterpieces often fail to meet the most important requirement—namely, the ability to float in a desirable manner when presented to the fish.

In my own effort to create a series of artificials possessing the most important characteristics of the natural insect, such as silhouette, translucency, and floatability, it became necessary to incorporate materials and tying methods rarely used. I do not mean to be disrespectful of the old masters or traditional fly-dressing procedures, but a little rule-bending has resulted in very realistic-looking dry-fly imitations that are fishable, durable, and extremely effective, and, perhaps best of all, they can be dressed by anyone who has mastered the fundamentals of fly-dressing.

While my love for creative fly dressings may seem to take priority in most of my work, it would be an unforgivable sin to dismiss the beautiful traditionals that have laid the foundation for fly tying through generations. Although they are not dealt with technically in this book, they are far from forgotten, and traditional patterns of note are mentioned with each of my dressings.

DRESSING THE MAYFLY DUN, STEP BY STEP

In the adult, whether we are concerned about the dun (subimago) or spinner (imago) stage, one mayfly doesn't differ much from another; at least for the purpose of tying and presenting the artificial to the fish, they are alike, and only the color, size, and type of material used is of concern. The three versions of dun dressings in this section can be tied by using the step-by-step instructions that follow.

Before getting started one would do well to study mayfly anatomy and get acquainted with the proportions and shapes and at the same time look into the material needed. As the anatomy drawing of the natural insect suggests, it's unmistakably one of the most beautiful insects found along the stream, one that is easy to identify by its shape. It is also deadly as a well-dressed artificial.

I have chosen *Isonychia* as the model for the instructions on how to dress all three versions, first because it's best not to work with the small flies at the outset of learning something new, and second because I am personally very fond of this large smoky-winged insect, which has given me much pleasure and enjoyment in taking some of my best "twilight fish."

The dry flies an angler decides to use, however, are a matter of personal choice, although he usually will choose those he has had good luck with and stick to them until something better comes along. The fish may not have any choice in this matter, but seem to be fooled as readily by a fly that floats on its fur body as by a traditional fly that floats on its hackle and has a fragile quill body and wood duck wings. I suppose it is fair to say that despite joining the "parachute hackle" fraternity, I still enjoy the dressing of traditional dries with the stiff natural hackles that are so hard to get—except perhaps in Harry Darbee's back yard. The most practical way of overcoming the difficulty of obtaining good stiff hackles for dry flies is to alter the design so the fly does not depend on its hackle to float. Then one can merely use a "fairly good" hackle wound directly around the wing to represent legs and stabilize the fly in natural upright position. The ones I have been using for years could easily be referred to as "three-in-one flies," dressed as a hair-wing for those who don't care to spend too much time at the vise, or as a cut-wing dun or realistic cut-wing for the angler who demands the ultimate in realism and delicacy and is willing to give great patience and devotion to the art.

Mayfly adult

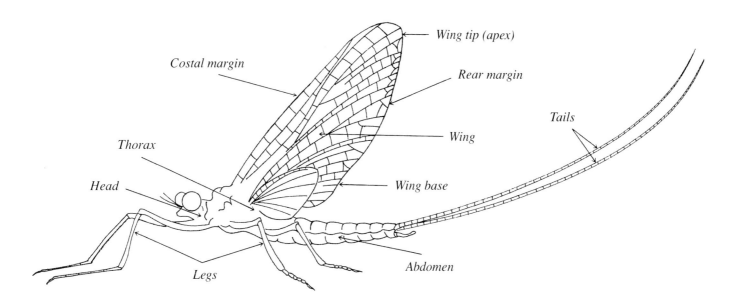

Anatomy of a mayfly adult

Isonychia Dun

Common Names	Dun Variant, White-Gloved Howdy, Leadwing Coachman
Genus	*Isonychia*
Species	*bicolor, sadleri*
Availability	Late afternoon and early evening from late May through August; East and Midwest.

Hair-Wing Dressing

Hook	Mustad 94842, size 10
Thread	Olive, prewaxed 6/0
Wings	Darkest-gray deer body hair; length, 16mm
Tails	Ginger hackle fibers, same length as the wings
Body	Dark-reddish-brown fur dubbing, fine-textured
Hackle	Dark-ginger cock hackle, tied parachute
Head	Olive tying thread
Dubbing Formula	4 parts medium brown, 2 parts black, and 1 part red

Cut-Wing Dressing

(Same dressing as above, except for wing)

Wings	Two blue dun rooster or hen body feathers trimmed to shape; length, 16mm

Realistic Dressing

Body Length	16mm
Hook	Mustad 94842, size 12
Thread	Olive, prewaxed 6/0
Extension	Mahogany-brown spade hackle with fibers drawn reversed and set in heavy tying cement; length, 8mm
Tails	Two fibers from extension material; length, 16mm
Wings	Same as cut-wing dressing
Thorax	Fur dubbing (same as hair-wing body); length, 8mm
Hackle	Same as hair-wing
Head	Same as hair-wing

Proportions

Before starting to dress these types of dry flies it should be noted that the proportions are somewhat different from those suggested for the traditionals. In the traditionals, the wings, tails, and body are of the same approximate size. The reason for the difference is simply to minimize the hook size, particularly for some of the larger artificials where the total body length would require extremely large hooks and thus affect their floating ability. The body length for hair-wing and cut-wing patterns is determined by the hook size that has been selected, which in some cases makes the fur body somewhat shorter than that of the natural—a circumstance that doesn't seem to decrease the effectiveness of the flies. The most important feature on a dry fly of this type is the wing length, which is why wing length is indicated in each pattern. The tails, while considered of minor importance on flies that float in their fur body, are the same length as the wings, unless otherwise indicated, and might well compensate for the lack in body length by suggesting the abdomen portion because of their raised position. The proportions may confuse you in the beginning and I suggest you make some small scale cards for the measurements most frequently used for the flies you will be tying. Realistic dressings have no body-length restrictions; they are made to closely coincide with the natural, as you will see in the instructions that follow.

Isonychia Dun (hair-wing)

Hook	Mustad 94842, size 10
Thread	Olive, prewaxed 6/0
Wings	Darkest-gray deer body hair; length, 16mm
Tails	Ginger hackle fibers, same length as the wings
Body	Dark-reddish-brown fur dubbing, fine-textured
Hackle	Dark-ginger cock hackle, tied parachute
Head	Olive tying thread
Dubbing Formula	4 parts medium brown, 2 parts black, and 1 part red

1. Cover the hook shank with tying thread as a foundation before taking it to where the wing is tied in, one-third of a hook length from the eye. Cut a small bunch of deer body hair from the skin and align the tips by pushing them through a funnel. The amount of hair needed depends on the size fly being dressed, but in this case it is about the diameter of a round toothpick when compressed lightly. Tie it in on top of the hook with the tips pointing forward over the eye. It is best to keep it on top if possible; it may flare a little, and if so, don't worry. A little flare is unavoidable. Now hold the butt ends firmly while you take several very tight turns of thread to the left, binding and compressing a small portion of the fibers to the hook shank.

2. Trim the butt ends to a long taper and wind your tying thread over them, forming a smooth, even underbody. Now take the tying thread forward to just behind the wing. Grasp all the fibers and hold them back while taking several turns of thread in front. Take some turns directly around the wing and build up a little pile of thread up the wing for a distance. There should be enough room between the uppermost windings on the wing and the hook shank to serve as a base for winding the hackle after the fur body has been applied. To keep the wing upright, take the turns directly around the wing first, then hold the thread parallel with the top of the shank, pulling lightly to the rear. When the wing sits in the desired position, spiral the thread around the shank, thus anchoring the wing in a perfect upright position. Apply some clear cement on the thread windings.

3. Tie in six to eight hackle fibers for the tail, which should be the same length as the wing. Do this in the same manner as if you were dressing a traditional dry fly. When they are secured, take several turns of thread directly around all the fibers, then raise them to a 45-degree angle and hold them there while pulling the thread tight and winding it around the shank, thus holding them in that position in the same way as when securing the wing. Apply some clear cement on the thread windings. Wind the thread to directly in front of the wing and tie in the hackle; the hackle should be pointing forward with the shiny side up.

4. Apply the fur body in regular dry-fly style. It should be dubbed to just behind the wing before taking one turn close to the front of the wing. Now hold the hackle to the rear and dub the front portion.

6. The fly can be left as it is with just a bunched upright wing, but if you wish, you can carefully trim away the center portion and create a divided and less dense set of wings, as shown above. When the fibers are cut away, I often apply some clear cement on the stumps and base of the wing fibers themselves for more strength.

5. Wind the hackle parachute-style directly around the base of the wing, making sure that each succeeding turn is beneath the previous one. Tie off in front and cut the surplus before winding a small head.

DRESSING THE CUT-WING ISONYCHIA DUN

Anglers will generally agree that the fly requirements for slow-moving pools and long, placid stretches of stream are very rigid and only flies that closely resemble the naturals are going to fool the fish. The importance of the wings on dry flies should not be taken lightly; it is my opinion that they are the most dominating feature on a well-designed artificial. I doubt if any other fly wings look more natural than those cut to shape from the delicate body feathers of a rooster or hen, and they are surprisingly durable.

Many of my angling friends have often objected to the wings and claim that they spin on the leader tippet. However, in most cases it is not the fault of the fly, but of a wrongly selected tippet. By observing the simple rule of dividing the hook size by three, you will arrive at the correct "X" number for your tippet and thus eliminate the possibility of spinning. But as you should know, even an oversized tippet can't prevent spinning if the wings are not set straight, and I strongly recommend that you take plenty of time to learn the method of setting the wings.

The difference between the hair-wing and the cut-wing appears to be a minor one, as only the wing makes the difference between the two, and yet, the wing preparation is extremely important and may seem time-consuming at first. However, it is quite simple once you get the hang of it and learn the proportions of those you use most often. The scale cards mentioned earlier would be a great help.

Isonychia Dun (cut-wing)

Hook	Mustad 94842, size 10
Thread	Olive, prewaxed 6/0
Wings	Two blue dun rooster or hen body feathers trimmed to shape; length, 16mm
Tails	Ginger hackle fibers, same length as the wings
Body	Dark-reddish-brown fur dubbing, fine-textured
Hackle	Dark-ginger cock hackle, tied parachute
Head	Olive tying thread
Dubbing Formula	4 parts medium brown, 2 parts black, and 1 part red

1. Select a pair of body feathers of the same size and shade. They should be firm and straight except for a small natural curvature throughout the stem. Pull off the fuzz and lower fibers and leave only enough on the stem for the size wing you are cutting (in this case 16mm). The lowest fibers on each side of the stem must be directly across from each other.

3. Hold the feather shiny side up and trim the front margin (front edge) to shape with a pair of large toenail clippers.

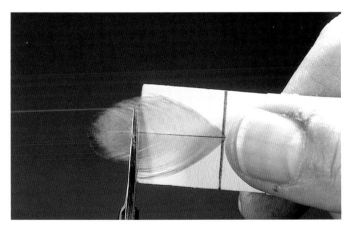

2. Mark the wing length on a small piece of cardboard with a pencil line, as suggested. Place the feather on the cardboard with the lower fibers directly at the pencil mark. Trim away the tip portion of both feathers, one at a time, and you have the total wing length.

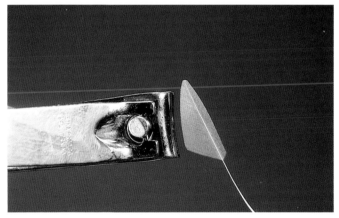

4. Turn the feather over and trim the costal margin (rear edge). (Note that it is trimmed closer to the stem in the front, offsetting it from the center for better balance.)

5. Make a second wing in the same manner, but hold the feather with the dull underside up when cutting the rear margin. Round the corners of the apex and rear margin at the wing base, and you have the two finished wings ready to be tied in. If cut correctly, the wider portion of the wings should project toward the rear when placed on the hook with their shiny sides together.

6. On this version the tail is tied in first, but in the same manner as explained for the hair-wing version. When properly set, wind the thread to a position one-third of a hook length from the eye, where the wings will be tied in. Apply a small amount of clear cement on the windings at the tail to affix it permanently.

7. If anything is of importance on this type of fly, it is fastening the cut wings. They must be secured with the fibers running absolutely parallel to the hook shank and sitting straight up in relation to the hook bend when viewed from the front. This may be troublesome at first, but I can assure you that there is no sense in finishing a fly that will spin like a propeller. The trick is to secure the wing stems side by side on top of the hook, then quickly raise both wings at the same time and actually kink the stems so that the wings stay almost straight up by themselves. When this is accomplished they are held together with several turns of tying thread directly around the small portion of bare upright wing stems. Hold the wings between your fingertips with the shiny sides together and perfectly aligned with one another. Straddle the hook shank with your fingertips and place the wings on top with the stems projecting forward over the eye. Take a couple of quick turns over the stems to hold them. Now adjust the wings so that there is a bit of clear stem between the lowest fibers and the first thread windings. (The small distance is for application of hackle legs later on.) Now secure the wing stems firmly on top of the hook shank. The stems are still on in the photographs; before proceeding, cut them just short of the hook eye.

8. Trim the hackle stems to just short of the hook eye and bind down the remainder with thread. Raise the wings together and secure them in an upright position with windings directly around the base of the wing stems and the hook shank. Apply some clear cement on the windings.

9. Make sure wings are positioned properly, as above.

10. Front view of properly set wings.

11. The fly is now completed in the same manner as explained for the hair-wing dressing, Steps 3, 4, and 5.

THE REALISTIC DRESSING

Realistic imitations of mayflies have never been fully explored, but I suspect the future will bring many fine innovative tying methods that will achieve the ultimate in fly design. At present there are but a few that can qualify as practical dressings; instead they sit safely on their mounts in a frame, well out of reach of slimy fish and greedy anglers who might dare to fish with them if given a chance. As a prizefighter watches his weight, the fly dresser must watch the weight of his artificials if they are to float on the surface as intended. The extra load of an extension may be too much, and the fly will be tail-heavy; or it is too fragile and will take but one fish before it is torn and useless.

The most practical method of forming the abdomen extension for realistic flies was discovered in the late 1950s when Harry Darbee, the celebrated American fly dresser of Livingston Manor, New York, discovered the "reverse-fiber" method: A single feather is held by the tip, and the rest of the fibers are pulled in reverse and crowded together closely along the stem, then set in lacquer to hold them in place. Harry generously let me use his method, which I wrote about in my book *Dressing Flies for Fresh and Salt Water,* and since then I have designed a list of dressings (Harry might have done the same if Elsie had locked him in his study). These patterns are fishable, durable, and not too difficult for the moderately accomplished tier. Forming the abdomen extension is by far the most difficult task in tying realistic mayflies. For a long time I struggled to find a method that was both practical and quick. Since regular fly-tying head cement is very thin, I didn't find it suitable as an adhesive for binding the fibers together, and for a long time I used clear nail polish, which is much thicker and dries fairly quickly.

Isonychia Dun (realistic)

Body Length	16mm
Hook	Mustad 94842, size 12
Thread	Olive, prewaxed 6/0
Extension	Mahogany-brown spade hackle with fibers drawn reversed and set in heavy tying cement, length, 8mm
Tails	Two fibers from extension material; length, 16mm
Wings	Same as cut-wing dressing
Thorax	Fur dubbing (same as hair-wing body); length, 8mm
Hackle	Same as hair-wing
Head	Same as hair-wing

Almost any hackle or body feather can be used for preparing the extension, but the feather I prefer is a rooster spade hackle, because it usually has a nice webby portion on the lower end and good stiff fibers in the tip section for the tails. In some cases it is hard to locate hackles with the necessary characteristics in color and size for a particular pattern, and some tinting may be called for, either by dying the feather or by touching it up with a Pantone waterproof marking pen.

1. For the *Isonychia* I have selected a mahogany-colored spade hackle with tip fibers of the same length as indicated in the dressing for tails (16mm). Stroke down the fibers below the tip section and pull them off on each side, leaving the rest on a 15mm portion on the stem as shown. (This measurement changes in relation to the size extension you are making.) The fibers nearest to the tip must be directly across from one another.

2. Brush a small amount of fairly thick tying cement on stems and fibers.

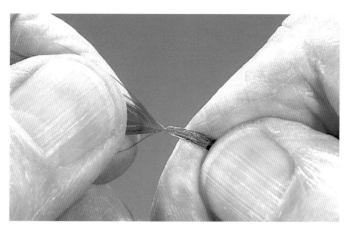

4. The compressed fibers must be drawn into final shape while the glue is still tacky. To do this, I place it in the first joint of my index finger with the dull side of the feather down and my thumb on top keeping it in place. (That, incidentally, is why you have a first joint on your index finger, just in case you didn't know.) Bend your finger slightly and draw the feather out slowly as many times as needed. This will fold the compressed fibers down a little on each side of the stem and form a V-shaped extension.

3. Hold the feather by the tip portion and draw it repeatedly out between your thumb and first finger. This will hold the fibers in reverse close to the stem. The extension will now appear to be rather flat with merely a natural curve.

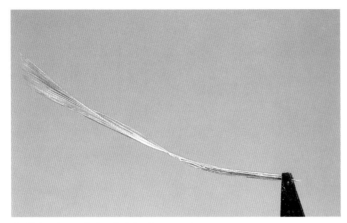

5. Side view of the finished extension.

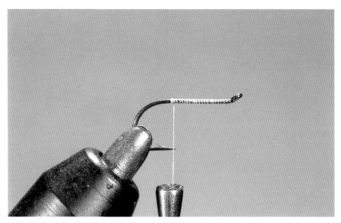

7. Attach the tying thread at the hook eye and wind it back to directly above the point of the hook. (Remember, the hook for the realistic dressing is smaller than that for the other two versions.) This is the tie-in spot of the extension and must be accurately positioned.

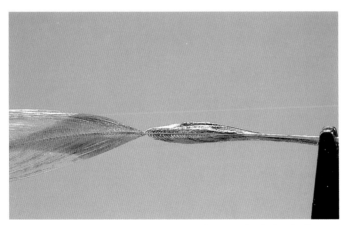

6. Top view of the extension. Set it aside and let it dry before you go any further. In the meantime, make a few extensions for later use. The first couple may not be to your liking, but they'll improve with practice.

8. Before tying in the extension, cut it to length—the distance between the tie-in position and the front of the hook eye, plus enough fiber and stem to fasten it to the hook (in this case, an extra $1/8$-inch). Apply a drop of clear cement on the hook and set the extension on top. Fasten it securely with thread, aligning it with the hook shank horizontally and the hook bend vertically.

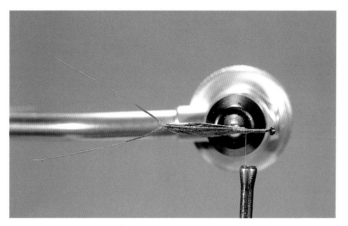

9. Separate the outer fibers on each side of the tip portion and hold them out of the way while trimming the center portion. Do not trim too close, but leave a bit of stump between the tails so that you can apply a little clear cement to strengthen the tail structure. If a three-tail abdomen is needed, leave two fibers on one side and one on the other. The third one can be centered when the cement is applied and kept in place while drying.

10. The abdomen extension must be fairly dry and well set before continuing the dressing. I have found it convenient to complete several abdomens and attach them to the hooks at the same time. Not only will you always need more than just one fly, but as you get into the swing of making the extensions, each one seems to get better than the preceding ones. The steps needed for completion of the Realistic Mayfly have already been explained in the instructions for the hair-wing and cut-wing, so they need not be repeated here. When applying the fur body, or thorax as it is called on the realistic, care must be taken to start the dubbing at the abdomen tie-in point and cover the thread windings. Start the dubbing procedure sparsely and make a smooth transition between the abdomen fibers and the thorax fur.

Simplified Abdomen Extension

There are times when the regular abdomen extension made with fibers drawn into shape is not practical, particularly on very small flies or when weight must be kept to an absolute minimum. For these occasions the simplified one might work better and is much simpler to make.

The characteristics of the feathers used are the same, but instead of drawing the fibers into shape, they are trimmed off, leaving only some small stumps that can then be set in silicone glue. When the glue is applied it is drawn through the fingers, holding it by the stem, thus setting the short fibers in the direction of the tall rather than reversed like the one previously explained. It should be noted that the trimming must be done in such a way that there is enough fiber left to make an extension that is wide enough for the particular insect you are copying. The simplified extension is by no means inferior but does not have the "full" look of the other one. While the regular type is better for most realistic dun dressings, the simplified type is by far better for the large spinners described later.

DRESSING THE MAYFLY SPINNER, STEP BY STEP

The spinners, or imagos as the entomologists call them, are the last stage in the life cycle of a mayfly. The insect has now changed from a rather dull-colored sub-imago to a bright, shiny spinner with almost glassy clear wings and somewhat longer tails than those of the duns. Some mayfly species change from duns to spinners almost immediately after hatching, such as those of the genera *Caenis (Tricorythodes)* and *Ephoron,* while others take as long as twenty-four hours to appear in their new attire, which means that you may often observe spinners of insects from the previous day's hatching, but by no means does this handiwork of nature make any difference when fishing the artificial spinner. The main difference between dun and spinner, as far as the fly tier is concerned, lies in the wing position. The dun is usually upright and slightly divided, whereas the spinner is spent or half-spent when it falls into the water when it reaches the last few moments of its life.

Isonychia Spinner

Hook	Mustad 94842, size 10
Thread	Olive, prewaxed 6/0
Tails	Four to six ginger hackle fibers, one and one-half times body length, dressed in an open V-shape
Wings	Pale gray or white SLF hank or poly yarn tied spent and trimmed
Body	Dark-reddish-brown fur dubbing
Dubbing Formula	Same as for the dun

1. Attach the tying thread and wind it back to a position above the barb. Apply a very small amount of fur on the tying thread and dub a small fur ball on the shank above the point of the hook barb. This fur will keep the tail fibers divided when tied in, and if kept small, will blend with the rest of the body.

3. Wind the tying thread to a position one third hook shank from the eye and tie in a small bunch of SLF hank fibers that are a bit longer than the finished wing. Fasten them securely with crisscross thread windings.

2. Select 6 stiff hackle fibers long enough to form a tail that is one and one half times the body length. Tie them in as a bunch close to the fur ball. Now press 3 fibers down on each side of the fur ball to form an open V-shape. Secure them in that fashion with tying thread close up against the ball. Apply a drop of tying cement on the windings.

4. Hold the wing fibers together above the hook and trim them to length at a slant as shown in the photo. They should be as long as one body length.

5. Fold the wings out to a spent position to each side and make sure the fibers are well spread. Now apply some cement on the thread windings and base of the fibers to hold them in position.

7. Front view of the fly. Note that the wings are slanting slightly upward,

6. Wind the tying thread back to directly in front of the fur ball. Apply some fur on the thread and form the body, criss-crossing it between the wings and finishing off in front. Form a small head with tying thread and tie it off. This finishes your spinner.

A little Caenis *spinner with wings of poly yarn. The female has a white abdomen and black thorax, the male a black abdomen and black thorax.*

Selected Mayfly Dun and Spinner Dressings

The dressings included in the list that follows are those most frequently used in different parts of the country, at least by me and by many of the more knowledgeable fishing friends who give me the pleasure of sharing a piece of water now and then, who are always first to admit the impossibility of selecting a conclusive list of dressings that work every time everywhere, and who are also first to admit that if failure strikes, I probably dressed their fly.

The author with his first grayling. It fell for a dark realistic dun.

To those who have favorite flies not found on the list, I apologize, but perhaps the preceding tying instructions will enable them to proceed on their own and establish new dressings that we all someday may enjoy.

You will note that in the dressing patterns spinner tails are often mentioned as being tied "straight back." This alternate method works for all spinners and is merely an ordinary traditional dry-fly tail arrangement.

Blue-Winged Hendrickson Dun

Common Names	Lady Beaverkill, Red Quill, Hendrickson
Genus	*Ephemerella*
Species	*subvaria*
Availability	Second week of April through May on

Eastern and Midwestern streams, starting in early afternoon.

Blue-Winged Hendrickson Dun (hair-wing)

Hook	Mustad 94842, size 12 to 14
Thread	Tan, prewaxed 6/0
Wings	Dark-gray deer body hair tips; wings: 13mm long
Tails	Small bunch of wood duck fibers; tails: 12mm long
Body	Creamish-pink fur dubbing
Hackle	Medium-blue-dun rooster hackle, tied parachute
Head	Tan tying thread
Dubbing Formula	In lieu of the urine-stained fur from a vixen, the darkest cream fox belly fur with medium pink added to give it a pinkish cast is acceptable

Blue-Winged Hendrickson Dun (cut-wing)

(Same as hair-wing except wings)

Wings	Two medium-blue-dun rooster body feathers trimmed to size; wings: 13mm long

Blue-Winged Hedrickson Dun (realistic)

Body Length	12mm
Hook	Mustad 94842, size 14
Thread	Tan, prewaxed 6/0
Extension	Small wood duck flank feather (light-colored) with fibers drawn reversed and set in silicone glue; extension: 6mm long; when extension is tied in, tint it lightly with pink Pantone 162M
Tails	Three fibers from extension material; tails: 12mm long
Wings	Same as cut-wing
Thorax	Fur dubbing (same as hair-wing body); thorax: 6mm long
Hackle	Same as hair-wing
Head	Same as hair-wing

Blue-Winged Hendrickson Spinner

Hook	Mustad 94842, size 12 to 14
Thread	Brown, prewaxed 6/0
Wings	Lightest-gray, hackle wound and tied spent; wings: 13mm long
Tails	Wood duck flank feather fibers tied open in V-shape or straight back; tails: 15mm long
Body	Medium-reddish-brown fur dubbing
Head	Brown tying thread
Dubbing Formula	2 parts medium brown, 1 part black, and 1 part red

Red Quill (traditional)

Hook	Mustad 94833, size 12 to 14
Thread	Black, prewaxed 6/0
Tails	Medium-blue-dun hackle fibers
Wings	Wood duck flank feather
Body	Reddish-brown hackle stem, stripped
Hackle	Medium-blue-dun rooster hackles
Head	Black tying thread

Dark Leptophlebia Dun

Common Names	Black Quill, Whirling Dun
Genus	*Leptophlebia*
Species	*cupida*
Availability	In the late morning through the afternoon

from late April through May in the East and Midwest.

Dark Leptophlebia Dun (hair-wing)

Hook	Mustad 94842, size 10 to 12
Thread	Black, prewaxed 6/0
Wings	Darkest-gray-brown deer body hair tips; wings: 14mm long
Tails	Dark-brown hackle fibers; tails: 15mm long
Body	Dark-reddish-brown fur dubbing
Hackle	Coch-y-bondhu rooster hackle, tied parachute
Head	Black tying thread
Dubbing Formula	3 parts dark brown and 1 part red

Dark Leptophlebia Dun (cut-wing)

(Same as hair-wing except wings)

Wings	Dark-rusty-blue-dun hen hackle or body feather (this can also be a dark-ginger-dyed blue dun if natural is not available) trimmed to shape; wings: 14mm long

Dark Leptophlebia Dun (realistic)

Body Length	14mm
Hook	Mustad 94842, size 12
Thread	Black, prewaxed 6/0
Extension	Coch-y-bondhu spade hackle or webby neck hackle from rooster or hen, with fibers drawn reversed and set in silicone glue; extension: 7mm long
Tails	Three fibers from extension material, center tail trimmed a little shorter than the outer ones; tails: 15mm long
Wings	Same as cut-wing
Thorax	Fur dubbing (same as hair-wing body); thorax: 7mm long
Hackle	Same as hair-wing
Head	Same as hair-wing

Dark Leptophlebia Spinner

Hook	Mustad 94842, size 10 to 12
Thread	Black, prewaxed 6/0
Wings	Medium-gray, tied spent; wings: 14mm long
Tails	Brown hackle fibers tied open V-shape or straight-back; tails: 17mm long
Body	Dark-reddish-brown dubbing
Head	Black tying thread
Dubbing Formula	Same as for the hair-wing dressing

Black Quill (traditional)

Hook	Mustad 94833, size 10 to 12
Thread	Black, prewaxed 6/0
Tails	Blackish-blue-dun hackle fibers
Wings	Black hackle tips
Body	Badger hackle stem, stripped
Hackle	Blackish-blue-dun rooster hackles
Head	Black tying thread

Golden Drake Dun

Common Names	Evening Dun, Cream Variant
Genus	*Potamanthus*
Species	*distinctus*
Availability	At twilight on Eastern and Midwestern

streams, from mid-June to the first week of August.

Golden Drake Dun (hair-wing)

Hook	Mustad 94842, size 10 to 12
Thread	Yellow, prewaxed 6/0
Wings	Pale-yellow-dyed deer body hair tips; wings: 16mm long
Tails	Pale-yellow hackle fibers; tails: 16mm long
Body	Pale-yellow fur dubbing
Hackle	Palest ginger rooster hackle, tied parachute
Head	Yellow tying thread
Dubbing Formula	Equal amounts of yellow and creamy white

Golden Drake Dun (cut-wing)

(Same as hair-wing except wings)

Wings	Palest-yellow-dyed rooster body feather or hen neck hackle trimmed to shape; wings: 16mm long

Golden Drake Dun (realistic)

Body Length	16mm
Hook	Mustad 94842, size 12
Thread	Yellow, prewaxed 6/0
Extension	Palest-yellow-dyed spade hackle with fibers drawn reversed and set in silicone glue; extension: 8mm long
Tails	Three fibers from the extension material; tails: 16mm long
Wings	Same as cut-wing
Thorax	Fur dubbing (same as for the hair-wing body); thorax: 8mm long
Hackle	Same as for hair-wing
Head	Same as for hair-wing

Golden Drake Spinner

Hook	Mustad 94842, size 10 to 12
Thread	Yellow, prewaxed 6/0
Wings	Palest-gray deer body hair tips tied spent; wings: 16mm long
Tails	Pale-yellow hackle fibers tied open V-shape or straight back; tails: 18mm long
Body	Pale-yellow fur dubbing (same as hair-wing dun)
Head	Yellow tying thread

Cream Variant (traditional)

Hook	Mustad 94833, size 10 to 12
Thread	Yellow, prewaxed 6/0
Tails	Cream hackle fibers, very stiff and fairly long
Wings	None
Body	Cream hackle stem, stripped
Hackle	Cream rooster neck or saddle hackle
Head	Yellow tying thread

Green Drake Dun (eastern)

Common Names	Green Drake, Coffin Fly
Genus	*Ephemera*
Species	*guttulata*
Availability	Last days of May through the first weeks of June, sporadically throughout the day and early evening hours.

Green Drake Dun (hair-wing)

Hook	Mustad 94842, size 10
Thread	Yellow, prewaxed 6/0
Wings	Well-marked grayish-brown deer body hair tips; wings: 22mm long
Tails	Three dark moose mane fibers; tails same length as wings
Body	Pale-creamish-yellow fur dubbing with an olive cast
Hackle	Golden badger rooster hackle, tied parachute
Head	Yellow tying thread
Dubbing Formula	3 parts creamy white, 1 part yellow with a pinch of medium olive to give an olive cast

Green Drake Dun (cut-wing)

(Same as hair-wing except for wings)

Wings	Two wood duck flank feathers, or two well-marked mallard flank feathers dyed chartreuse, trimmed to shape; wings: 22mm long

Green Drake Dun (realistic)

Body Length	22mm
Hook	Mustad 94842, size 10
Thread	Yellow, prewaxed 6/0
Extension	Mallard flank feather dyed pale creamish-yellow with a pinch of olive added; fibers drawn reversed and set in silicone glue; optional back marking can be applied with a brown Pantone marker; extension: 11mm long
Tails	Three fibers from extension material; tails: 22mm long
Wings	Sam as cut-wing
Thorax	Fur dubbing (same as for hair-wing body); thorax: 11mm long
Hackle	Same as hair-wing dressing
Head	Yellow tying thread

Green Drake Spinner

Hook	Mustad 94842, size 10
Thread	White, prewaxed 6/0
Wings	Grizzly hackle, wound and tied; wings: 22mm long
Tails	Three dark moose mane fibers tied straight back; tails: 28mm long
Body	Creamy White fur dubbing
Head	White tying thread
Dubbing Formula	white fur

Note: This spinner is a good candidate for a simplified extension made from a creamy white spade hackle. The tails are then tinted with a dark brown Pantone marker.

White Wulff (traditional)

Hook	Mustad 94833, size 10
Thread	White, prewaxed 6/0
Tails	White calf tail
Wings	White calf tail
Body	Creamy white fur or yarn
Hackle	Golden badger
Head	White tying thread

Gray Fox Dun

Common Names	Gray Fox, Ginger Quill
Genus	*Stenonema*
Species	*fuscum*
Availability	Start to hatch in midmorning on some

waters and late in the day on others; found in East and Midwest from mid-May through June.

Gray Fox Dun (hair-wing)

Hook	Mustad 94842, size 12 to 14
Thread	Yellow, prewaxed 6/0
Wings	Well-marked grayish-brown deer body hair tips; wings: 14mm long
Tails	Small bunch of wood duck fibers; tails: 12mm long
Body	Yellowish-tan fur dubbing
Hackle	One light ginger and one grizzly, wound together (a grizzly dyed light tan may be used, in which case only one hackle is needed)
Head	Yellow tying thread
Dubbing Formula	1 part medium brown, 1 part yellow, and 1 part cream

Gray Fox Dun (cut-wing)

(Same as hair-wing except for wings)

Wings	Two gray partridge body feathers trimmed to shape; wings: 14mm long

Gray Fox Dun (realistic)

Body Length	12mm
Hook	Mustad 94842, size 14
Thread	Yellow, prewaxed 6/0
Extension	Pale-ginger spade hackle with fibers drawn reversed and set in silicone glue; optional back markings, brown Pantone 154M; extension material; tails: 6mm long
Tails	Two fibers from the extension material; tails: 12mm long
Wings	Same as cut-wing
Thorax	Fur dubbing (same as hair-wing body; length, 6mm)
Hackle	Same as hair-wing
Head	Same as hair-wing

Gray Fox Spinner

Hook	Mustad 94842, size 12 to 14
Thread	Yellow, prewaxed 6/0
Wings	Lightest-gray hackle wound and tied spent; wings: 14mm long
Tails	Wood duck flank feather fibers tied open V-shape or straight back; tails: 15mm long
Body	Yellowish-amber fur dubbing
Head	Yellow tying thread
Dubbing Formula	2 parts cream, 1 part medium reddish-brown, and 1 part yellow

Gray Fox (traditional)

Hook	Mustad 94833, size 12 to 14
Thread	Yellow, prewaxed 6/0
Tails	Ginger hackle fibers
Wings	Mallard flank feather
Body	Light-fawn-colored fox fur
Hackle	Light ginger and grizzly wound together
Head	Yellow tying thread

Caenis Dun

Common Names	Angler's Curse,
	Tiny White-Winged Dun, Trico
Genus	*Tricorythodes*
Species	Various
Availability	Midmorning hours from June through

September and early October; found throughout the country.

Male Caenis Dun

Hook	Mustad 94842, size 22 to 28
Thread	Black, prewaxed 6/0
Tails	Light-blue-dun hackle fibers,
	dressed in an open V-shape
Wings	Small bunch of white poly yarn set upright
Body	Very sparse black fur dubbing, heaviest
	black fur dubbing, heaviest near the wing
Hackle	None

Note: Because of its size, the hackle is omitted and the tails are tied in an open V-shape and are not raised as is customary on most of the other patterns. The outrigger type of tail construction will stabilize the fly, which in this case floats directly on its fur body with the aid of dry-fly flotant.

A size 22 female Caenis *spinner.*

Female Caenis Spinner

Hook	Mustad 94842, size 22 to 28
Thread	Black, prewaxed 6/0
Tails	Three light-blue-dun fibers tied straight back, fairly long
Wings	White poly yarn, wound and tied spent, or just trimmed top and bottom
Abdomen	Light moose mane hair
Thorax	Black fur dubbing
Head	Black tying thread

Note: This fly is more important in the area where I fish than the dun, but I recommend that you watch closely to determine on which the fish are feeding.

Iron Blue Dun

Common Names	Gordon Quill, Quill Gordon, Iron Dun
Genus	*Epeorus*
Species	*pleuralis*
Availability	Early afternoon from mid-April through May, East and Midwest.

Iron Blue Dun (hair-wing)

Hook	Mustad 94842, size 12 to 14
Thread	Olive, prewaxed 6/0
Wings	Dark-gray deer body hair tips; wings: 11mm long
Tails	Small bunch of wood duck fibers; tails same length as wings
Body	Grayish-yellow fur dubbing
Hackle	Rusty-blue-dun rooster hackle, tied parachute
Head	Olive tying thread
Dubbing Formula	2 parts medium brown, 2 parts yellow, and 1 part gray beaver

Iron Blue Dun (cut-wing)

(Same as hair-wing except for wings)

Wings	Two medium-blue-dun rooster body feathers trimmed to shape; wings: 11mm long

Iron Blue Dun (realistic)

Body Length	11mm
Hook	Mustad 94842, size 14
Thread	Olive, prewaxed 6/0
Extension	A small wood duck flank feather with fibers drawn reversed and set in silicone glue; extension is sometimes tinted with yellow Pantone 115M if too light; extension: 6mm long
Tails	Two fibers from extension material; tails: 11mm long
Wings	Same as cut-wing
Thorax	Fur dubbing (same as hair-wing body); thorax: 5mm long
Hackle	Same as hair-wing
Head	Same as hair-wing

Iron Blue Spinner

Hook	Mustad 94842, size 12 to 14
Thread	Olive, prewaxed 6/0
Wings	Palest-grayish-tan hackle, wound and tied spent; wings: 11mm long
Tails	Medium-blue-dun hackle fibers tied open V-shape or straight back; tails: 15mm long
Body	Same as hair-wing
Head	Olive tying thread

Note: Suitable for simplified extension, in which case thorax is tinted to match the ginger-colored feather used for the extension. It is best to use a size 14 hook in this case.

Quill Gordon (traditional)

Hook	Mustad 94833, size 12 to 14
Thread	Olive, prewaxed 6/0
Tails	Medium-blue-dun hackle fibers
Wings	Wood duck flank feather
Body	Stripped quill from the eye of a peacock feather, bleached
Hackle	Medium-rusty-blue-dun rooster hackle

Light Cahill Dun

Common Names	Ginger Quill, Cahill, Light Cahill
Genus	*Stenonema*
Species	*canadense, ithaca*
Availability	Hatching sporadically throughout the day on Eastern and Midwestern waters from beginning of June through July.

Light Cahill Dun (hair-wing)

Hook	Mustad 94842, size 12 to 14
Thread	Yellow, prewaxed 6/0
Wings	Light-gray deer body hair tips; wings: 12mm long
Tails	Small bunch of pale wood duck fibers; tails same length as wings
Body	Creamish-tan fur dubbing
Hackle	Palest ginger hackle, tied parachute
Head	Yellow tying thread
Dubbing Formula	3 parts yellowish cream and 1 part light tan

Light Cahill (cut-wing)

(Same as hair-wing except for wings)

Wings	Two small wood duck flank feathers or pale-mottled-tan hen neck hackle trimmed to shape; wings: 12mm long

Light Cahill (realistic)

Body Length	11mm
Hook	Mustad 94842, size 14
Thread	Yellow, prewaxed 6/0
Extension	Yellowish-tan body feather of hen neck hackle, with fibers drawn reversed and set in silicone glue; extension: 6mm long
Tails	Two fibers from extension material; tails: 12mm long
Wings	Same as cut-wing
Thorax	Fur dubbing (same as for the hair-wing body); thorax: 5mm long
Hackle	Same as hair-wing
Head	Same as hair-wing

Light Cahill Spinner

Hook	Mustad 94842, size 12 to 14
Thread	Yellow, prewaxed 6/0
Wings	Palest-gray hackle wound and tied spent; wings: 12mm long
Tails	Light ginger hackle fibers tied open V-shape, or straight back; tails: 15mm long
Body	Creamish-tan fur dubbing (use hair-wing dubbing formula)
Head	Yellow tying thread

Light Cahill (traditional)

Hook	Mustad 94833, size 12 to 14
Thread	Yellow, prewaxed 6/0
Tails	Light-ginger hackle fibers
Wings	Palest wood duck flank feather
Body	Cream fur dubbing
Hackle	Very light ginger
Head	Yellow tying thread

Little Blue Mayfly

Common Names	Blue Quill, Blue Dun
Genus	*Paraleptophlebia*
Species	*adoptiva*
Availability	From noon through the day, from mid-April through May, East and Midwest.

Little Blue Mayfly (hair-wing)

Hook	Mustad 94842, size 18 to 20
Thread	Darkest-gray deer body hair tips; wings: 7mm long
Tails	Brown hackle fibers, same length as wings
Body	Dark reddish brown with an olive cast
Hackle	Medium-blue-dun rooster hackle tied parachute
Head	Brown tying thread
Dubbing Formula	3 parts dark brown, 1 part red, and 1 part medium olive

Note: I sometimes use deer body hair that has been dyed dark gray for the wings, but only when it's absolutely necessary.

Little Blue Mayfly (cut-wing)

(Same as hair-wing except for wings)

Wings	Darkest-blue-gray rooster body feathers trimmed to shape (for these small sizes I often use hen neck hackle instead); wings: 7mm long

Little Blue Mayfly (realistic)

Body Length	7mm
Hook	Mustad 94842, size 20
Thread	Brown, prewaxed 6/0
Extension	Simplified type; dark-reddish-brown hen hackle; extension: 4mm long
Tails	Three fibers from extension material; tails: 7mm long
Wings	Same as cut-wing
Thorax	Fur dubbing, very sparse (same as hair-wing body)
Hackle	Same as hair-wing
Head	Same as hair-wing

Little Blue Mayfly Spinner

Hook	Mustad 94842, size 18 to 20
Thread	Brown, prewaxed 6/0
Wings	Palest-grayish-tan hackle, wound, tied spent; wings: 7mm long
Tails	Pale-blue-dun hackle fibers, tied straight back; tails: 10mm long
Body	Same as for hair-wing
Head	Brown tying thread

Dark Red Quill (traditional)

Hook	Mustad 94833, size 18
Thread	Black, prewaxed 6/0
Tails	Dark-blue-gray hackle fibers
Wings	Two dark-blue-gray hackle tips
Body	Reddish-brown hackle stem, stripped
Hackle	Very dark blue-gray dun
Head	Black tying thread

Little Blue-Winged Baetis Dun

Common Name	Blue-Winged Olive
Genus	*Baetis*
Species	Various
Availability	Throughout country from April through October.

Little Blue-Winged Baetis Dun (hair-wing)

Hook	Mustad 94842, size 16 to 24
Thread	Olive, prewaxed 6/0
Wings	Medium-gray deer body hair tips; wings one body length long
Tails	Medium-blue-dun hackle fibers; tails same length as wings
Body	Medium-brown, or medium-olive, or medium-olive-brown fur dubbing
Hackle	Medium-blue-dun or grizzly, tied parachute
Head	Olive tying thread
Dubbing Formula	The first two dubbings are straight base colors; the third is equal parts of medium brown and medium olive

Note: I sometimes omit the parachute-type hackle, and instead tie the hackle in at the tail before the body is dubbed, then spiral a few turns forward to the front and tie off (open palmer style). When hackle is applied I trim off all the fibers under the fly.

Little Blue-Winged Baetis Dun (cut-wing)

(Same as hair-wing dressing, except for wings)

Wings	Medium-blue-gray hen hackle feathers trimmed to shape, and as long as one hook length

Little Blue-Winged Baetis Dun (realistic)

Since we are dealing with very small artificials in this instance, it's not practical to dress a full-fledged realistic. However, some added realism can be achieved by replacing the tail fibers with a simplified extension. In that case, use one size smaller hook than intended for the regular dressing, and needless to say, they are dressed with a set of fine cut wings.

Little Blue-Winged Baetis Spinner

Hook	Mustad 94842, size 16 to 24
Thread	Olive, prewaxed 6/0
Wings	Palest-gray hackle, wound and tied spent; wings one body length long
Tails	Medium-blue-dun hackle fibers tied straight back, very stiff
Body	Medium or dark brown, or medium reddish-brown (dark chestnut)
Head	Olive tying thread

Little Sulphur Dun

Common Names	Little Marryatt, Pale Evening Dun, Cut-Wing Sulphur Dun
Genus	*Ephemerella*
Species	*dorothea*
Availability	Late in the day or early evening in the East and Midwest, from middle of May to the first week of July.

Little Sulphur Dun (hair-wing)

Hook	Mustad 94842, size 16 to 18
Thread	Yellow, prewaxed 6/0
Wings	Medium-gray deer body hair tips; wings: 8mm long
Tails	Light-ginger hackle fibers, same length as wings
Body	Sulphur-yellow fur dubbing
Hackle	Very pale ginger, tied parachute
Head	Yellow tying thread
Dubbing Formula	4 parts bright yellow, 1 part cream, and 1 part medium olive

Little Sulphur Dun (cut-wing)

(Same as hair-wing except for wings)

Wings	Very-light-blue-dun body feather or hen hackle, trimmed to shape; wings: 8mm long

Little Sulphur Dun (realistic)

Body Length	8mm
Hook	Mustad 94842, size 18
Thread	Yellow, prewaxed 6/0
Extension	Small hen hackle or body feather dyed sulphur yellow, with fibers drawn reversed and set in silicone glue (or simplified extension of the same color); extension: 4mm long
Tails	Three fibers from extension material; tails: 8mm long
Wings	Same as cut-wing
Thorax	Fur dubbing (same as hair-wing body); thorax: 4mm long
Hackle	Same as hair-wing
Head	Same as hair-wing

Little Sulphur Spinner

Hook	Mustad 94842, size 16 to 18
Thread	Yellow, prewaxed 6/0
Wings	Palest-gray hackle, wound and tied spent; wings: 8mm long
Tails	Palest-blue-dun hackle fibers tied open V-shape or straight back; tails: 12mm long
Body	Yellowish-amber fur dubbing
Head	Yellow tying thread
Dubbing Formula	1 part chestnut brown, 1 part yellow, and 3 parts cream

Pale Evening Dun (traditional)

Hook	Mustad 94833, size 16 to 18
Thread	Yellow, prewaxed 6/0
Tails	Palest-ginger hackle fibers
Wings	Pale-blue-dun hackle tips
Body	Creamish-yellow fur dubbing
Hackle	Palest-ginger hackle
Head	Yellow tying thread
Dubbing Formula	Equal parts cream and yellow, fine-textured fur

March Brown Dun (American)

Common Names	Ginger Quill, Brown Drake, March Brown
Genus	*Stenonema*
Species	*vicarium*
Availability	Sporadically during the day from mid-May through June, East and Midwest.

March Brown Dun (hair-wing)

Hook	Mustad 94842, size 10 to 12
Thread	Yellow, prewaxed 6/0
Wings	Well-marked grayish-brown deer body hair tips; wings: 16mm long
Tails	Small bunch of wood duck fibers; tails: 14mm long
Body	Yellowish-amber fur dubbing
Hackle	One grizzly and one dark ginger wound together, parachute-style (a grizzly dyed medium brown will give the same result, in which case only one hackle is used)
Head	Yellow
Dubbing Formula	2 parts cream, 1 part medium reddish-brown, and 1 part yellow

March Brown Dun (cut-wing)

(Same as hair-wing, excet for wings)

Wings	Two mottled brown back feathers from ringneck pheasant, trimmed to shape (these feathers are located right at the root of the tail feathers); wings: 16mm long

March Brown Dun (realistic)

Body Length	15mm
Hook	Mustad 94842, size 12
Thread	Yellow, prewaxed 6/0
Extension	Yellowish-tan spade hackle, or yellow breast feather from ringneck pheasant, with fibers reversed and set in silicone glue (optional back markings made with a brown Pantone 154M); extension: 8mm long
Tails	Two fibers from extension material; tails: 14mm long
Wings	Same as cut-wing
Thorax	Fur dubbing (same as hair-wing body); thorax: 7mm long
Hackle	Same as hair-wing
Head	Same as hair-wing

March Brown Spinner

Hook	Mustad 94842, size 10 to 12
Thread	Yellow, prewaxed 6/0
Wings	Lightest-gray hackle, wound and tied spent; wings: 16mm long
Tails	Wood duck flank feather fibers tied open V-shape or straight back; tails: 18mm long
Body	Yellowish-brown fur dubbing
Dubbing Formula	2 parts medium brown, 1 part cream, and 1 part yellow

American March Brown (traditional)

Hook	Mustad 94833, size 10 to 12
Thread	Orange, prewaxed 6/0
Tails	Dark-ginger hackle fibers
Wings	Well-marked wood duck flank feather
Body	Light fawn-colored fox fur
Hackle	Grizzly and dark ginger wound together
Head	Orange tying thread

Medium Blue-Winged Olive

Common Names	Blue-Winged Olive, Small Dun Variant
Genus	*Ephemerella*
Species	*attenuata*
Availability	Midmorning on Eastern streams, from late May through June.

Medium Blue-Winged Olive (hair-wing)

Hook	Mustad 94842, size 16 to 18
Thread	Olive, prewaxed 6/0
Wings	Darkest-gray deer body hair tips (sometimes dyed dark gray); wings: 8mm long
Tails	Golden badger hackle fibers; same length as wings
Body	Yellowish-olive fur dubbing
Hackle	Golden badger rooster neck hackle, tied parachute
Head	Olive tying thread
Dubbing Formula	2 parts medium olive, 1 part yellow, and 1 part gray beaver

Medium Blue-Winged Olive (cut-wing)

(Same as hair-wing except for wings)

Wings	Two blue-gray rooster body feathers trimmed to size; wings: 8mm long

Medium Blue-Winged Olive (realistic)

Body Length	8mm
Hook	Mustad 94842, size 18
Thread	Olive, prewaxed 6/0
Extension	Small hen hackle or body feather dyed yellowish-olive, with fibers drawn reversed and set in silicone glue (a simplified extension-type may also be used instead); extension: 4mm long
Tails	Three fibers from extension material; tails: 8mm long
Wings	Same as cut-wing
Thorax	Fur dubbing (same as hair-wing body); thorax: 4mm long
Hackle	Same as hair-wing
Head	Same as hair-wing

Medium Blue-Winged Olive Spinner

Hook	Mustad 94842, size16 to 18
Thread	Olive, prewaxed 6/0
Wings	Palest-gray hackle wound and tied spent; wings: 8mm long
Tails	Golden badger hackle fibers tied open V-shape, or three very stiff fibers tied straight back; tails: 10mm long
Body	Dark olive-brown dubbing
Head	Olive tying thread
Dubbing Formula	2 parts dark brown and 1part medium olive

Blue-Winged Olive (traditional)

Hook	Mustad 94833, size 16 to 18
Thread	Olive, prewaxed 6/0
Tails	Medium-blue-dun hackle fibers
Wings	Two dark-blue-dun hackle tips
Body	Yellowish-olive fur dubbing
Hackle	Medium blue dun
Dubbing Formula	2 parts medium olive, 1 part yellow, and 1 part gray beaver

Michigan Mayfly Dun

Common Names	Michigan Caddis, Fish Fly, Grizzly Wulff
Genus	*Hexagenia*
Species	*limbata*
Availability	At twilight from mid-June through July, Midwest.

Michigan Mayfly Dun (hair-wing)

Hook	Mustad 94842, size 10
Thread	Olive, prewaxed 6/0
Extension	Light-ginger spade hackle prepared as a simplified extension; extension: 20mm long
Tails	Two fibers from extension material; tails: 22mm long
Wings	Good amount of medium-gray deer body hair tips, set upright with center trimmed out for double-wing appearance; wings: 30mm long
Thorax	Yellowish-tan fur dubbing; thorax: 10mm long
Hackle	One grizzly and one ginger wound together, parachute-style
Head	Olive tying thread
Dubbing Formula	2 parts medium brown, 1 part yellow, and 1 part gray beaver

Michigan Mayfly Dun (realistic)

Body Length	30mm
Hook	Mustad 94842, size 10
Thread	Olive, prewaxed 6/0
Extension	Wood duck flank feather with fibers reversed and set in silicone glue (if extension is too light when finished, tint it to a yellowish-tan with Pantone marker; optional back markings are made with a purplish-brown Pantone 438M); extension: 20mm long
Tails	Two fibers from the extension material; tails: 22mm long
Wings	Two medium-blue-dun rooster body feathers trimmed to shape; wings: 30mm long
Thorax	Fur dubbing (use hair-wing formula)
Hackle	Same as hair-wing
Head	Same as hair-wing

Michigan Mayfly Spinner

Hook	Mustad 94842, size 10
Thread	Olive, prewaxed 6/0
Extension	Ginger-colored spade hackle prepared as extension; extension: 20mm long
Tails	Two fibers from extension material; tails: 25mm long
Wings	Two light-gray hackle wound and tied half-spent; wings: 30mm long
Thorax	Tan fur dubbing
Head	Olive tying thread

Grizzly Wulff (traditional)

Hook	Mustad 94833, size 6
Thread	Black, prewaxed 6/0
Tails	Brown calf tail
Wings	Brown calf tail
Body	Pale-yellow floss, lacquered
Hackle	Brown and grizzly, interwound
Head	Black

White-Winged Ephoron Dun

Common Names	White Fly, White Miller
Genus	*Ephoron*
Species	*leukon*

Availability   On some Eastern and Midwestern streams at twilight, during the months of August and September. The Potomac River in Maryland has blizzard hatches of the *Ephoron* genus the last two weeks of July, but of a species much larger than *leukon* and dressed on size 8 to 10 hooks. I use the same dressing for both flies.

White-Winged Ephoron Dun (hair-wing)

Hook	Mustad 94842, size 14
Thread	White, prewaxed 6/0
Wings	White deer body hair tips; wings: 12mm long
Tails	Pale-blue-dun hackle fibers; tails: 12mm long
Body	White fur dubbing
Hackle	Creamy-white rooster hackle, tied parachute
Head	White tying thread

White-Winged Ephoron Dun (cut-wing)

(Same as hair-wing, except for wings)

Wings	Two creamy-white rooster body feathers trimmed to shape; wings: 12mm long

White-Winged Ephoron Dun (realistic)

Body Length	12mm
Hook	Mustad 94842, size 16
Thread	White, prewaxed 6/0
Extension	Small white spade hackle with fibers drawn reversed and set in silicone glue; extension: 6mm long
Tails	Three fibers from extension material; tails: 12mm long
Wings	Same as cut-wing
Thorax	White fur dubbing; thorax: 6mm long
Hackle	Same as hair-wing
Head	Same as hair-wing

White-Winged Ephoron Spinner

Hook	Mustad 94842, size 14
Thread	White, prewaxed 6/0
Wings	White hackle, wound and tied spent; wings: 12mm long
Tails	Palest-blue-dun hackle fibers tied open V-shape or straight back; tails: 16mm long
Body	White fur dubbing
Head	White tying thread

White Miller (traditional)

Hook	Mustad 94833, size 8 to 14
Thread	White, prewaxed 6/0
Tails	White hackle fibers
Wings	White duck quill sections set upright
Body	White fur dubbing
Hackle	White rooster hackle
Head	White

Chapter 5
Caddisflies

Perhaps the most significant development in trout fishing is an all-out study of caddisflies in their various stages of development. While imitations of the Trichoptera have been around for many years, they have always been treated as second-class citizens and used only in dire emergencies. But caddisflies are more common for longer periods of time than even the precious mayfly on most streams.

In their underwater habitat the caddisflies differ from mayflies and stoneflies in both appearance and development. After hatching from the egg they appear as wormlike larvae that, after completion of growth, change into a pupal stage and remain as such for a couple of weeks or longer, depending on the species, after which they rise to the surface and emerge as winged adults. Some caddis larvae are often referred to as caddis worms and move about freely without any visible protection, while others build a protective case of underwater fragments such as leaves, small sticks, and fine sand.

DRESSING THE CADDIS LARVA, STEP BY STEP
The little wormlike caddis larvae vary in size from 4mm to 16mm in length and have the appearance of a slim cylindrical worm with a dark-brownish thorax and a dirty-colored abdomen. They are found throughout America; many streams and ponds are blessed with a number of species that can provide good fishing all season long. To determine the size and color of the larvae in the area you are fishing, it is fairly simple to count them. They are usually found on the rocky stream bottom and between stones in fairly shallow water.

The caddis larvae are not complicated to make, and the patterns I use are not given entomological classification, but merely represent a long list of different species found in our fishing waters.

For many years I have used different kinds of fur for the abdomen of my caddis larvae and fished them with good results throughout the country. But nothing can beat latex for effectiveness and ease of dressing. Raleigh Boaze, Jr., of Brunswick, Md., discovered the use of latex as a super material for his "Ral's Caddis," a series of artificials that after a short while have become the center of attention in the angling world. What Raleigh didn't know was that he had opened a whole new chapter in American fly-dressing with his discovery, which once again proves that a fly tier never graduates. The series of caddis larva imitations in this book are those of the old design, but the abdomen portion now incorporates Raleigh's latex material tinted with Pantone markers that are keyed to the color of each larva. All the patterns are dressed alike on a Mustad 3906 hook, which has a sproat bend that permits you to start the abdomen portion midway down the bend to incorporate a sight curve in the artificial. Since the normal habitat of the larva is at the bottom of the stream, they must be fished deep and will require additional weight, which is added by winding some .010 lead wire on the shank before the latex is wound on.

The larva I am using as a model for the dressing instructions is the celebrated Green Caddis Larva. Like so many other specimens I use as models, it was collected on the Beaverkill in the Catskills. The imitation is being dressed on a Mustad 3906 size 10, which is about the average size.

Green Caddis Larva

Hook	Mustad 3906, size 8 to 18
Thread	Brown, prewaxed 6/0
Underbody	Tying thread and .010 lead wire
Abdomen	Natural latex strip, $^3/_{32}$-inch wide, tinted
Thorax	Darkest-brown-dyed rabbit fur with guard hair mixed and spun in a loop
Legs	Underside of thorax fur left long and picked out
Head	Brown tying thread
Tinting	Abdomen: green Pantone 347M

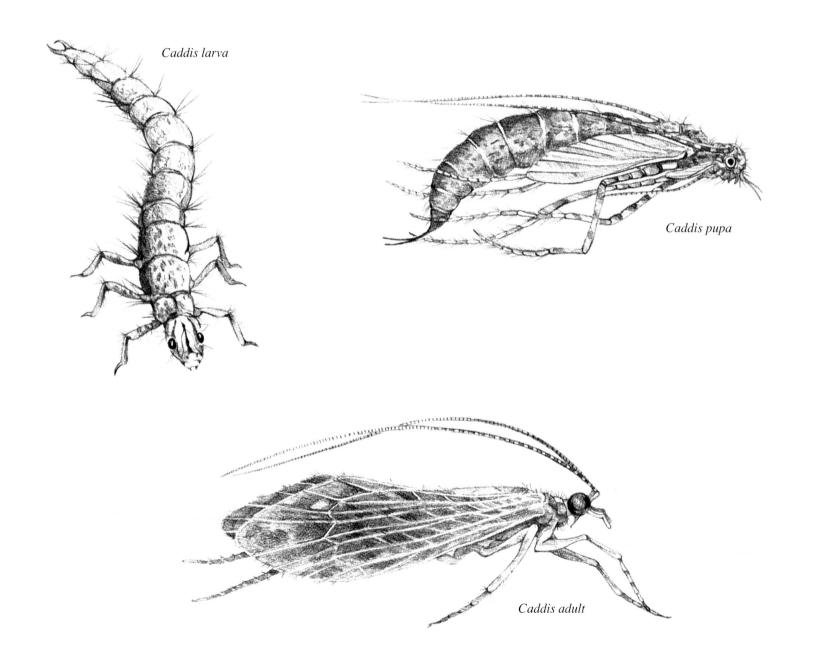

Caddis larva

Caddis pupa

Caddis adult

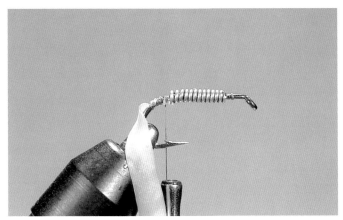

1. Wind the entire hook shank with tying thread and tie in the tapered end of a latex strip midway down on the bend. Wind the .010 lead wire neatly with turns closely side by side on a portion of the shank as seen. Before you wind the latex the wire should be completely covered with typing thread to form a smooth, even underbody.

3. Form a 3-inch spinning loop and spin a small amount of the thorax fur into a dubbing.

2. With very little stretch, wind the latex strip forward over the underbody in such a way that each turn overlaps the previous one by half its width. This produces the segmented effect that is characteristic of the natural larva. Secure the latex in front about a fourth of a body length from the eye with thread windings and cut the surplus latex.

4. Apply a small amount of clear cement on the shank and wind the dubbing on the thorax portion and tie off in front. Cut the surplus dubbing and trim the thorax on top and both sides with your scissors. The underside is picked out a little more to represent the legs. Add some clear cement on the head and tint the abdomen portion with a Pantone marker.

Selected Larva Dressings

White Caddis Larva

Hook	Mustad 3906, size 8 to 18
Thread	Brown, prewaxed 6/0
Underbody	Tying thread and .010 lead wire
Abdomen	Natural latex strip, $^3/_{32}$-inch wide
Thorax	Darkest-brown-dyed rabbit fur with hair mixed and spun in a loop
Legs	Underside of thorax left long and picked out
Head	Brown tying thread
Tinting	None

Gray Caddis Larva

Hook	Mustad 3906, size 8 to 18
Thread	Brown, prewaxed 6/0
Underbody	Tying thread and .010 lead wire
Abdomen	Natural latex strip, $^3/_{32}$-inch wide, tinted
Thorax	Darkest-brown-dyed rabbit fur with guard hair mixed and spun in a loop
Legs	Underside of thorax left long and picked out
Head	Brown tying thread
Tinting	Abdomen: gray Pantone 413M

Olive Caddis Larva

Hook	Mustad 3906, size 8 to 18
Thread	Brown, prewaxed 6/0
Underbody	Tying thread and .010 lead wire
Abdomen	Natural latex strip, $^3/_{32}$-inch wide, tinted
Thorax	Darkest-brown-dyed rabbit fur with guard hair mixed and spun in a loop
Legs	Underside of thorax left long and picked out
Head	Brown tying thread
Tinting	Abdomen: yellow-olive Pantone 104M

Orange Caddis Larva

Hook	Mustad 3906, size 8 to 18
Thread	Brown, prewaxed 6/0
Underbody	Tying thread and .010 lead wire
Abdomen	Natural latex strip, $^3/_{32}$-inch wide, tinted
Thorax	Darkest-brown rabbit fur with guard hair mixed and spun in a loop
Legs	Underside of thorax fur left long and picked out
Head	Brown tying thread
Tinting	Abdomen: orange Pantone 150M

Yellow Caddis Larva

Hook	Mustad 3906, size 8 to 18
Thread	Brown, prewaxed 6/0
Underbody	Tying thread and .010 lead wire
Abdomen	Natural latex strip, $^3/_{32}$-inch wide, tinted
Thorax	Darkest-brown-dyed rabbit fur with guard hair mixed and spun in a loop
Legs	Underside of thorax fur left long and picked out
Head	Brown tying thread
Tinting	Abdomen: yellow Pantone 115M

DRESSING THE CADDIS PUPA, STEP BY STEP

The most vulnerable time in a caddisfly's life is when it terminates the lease on its protective shelter built of sand, small stones, sticks, and other debris, in which it has remained enclosed for the duration of pupation. It must now swim to the surface and appear in its adult stage. During the final journey to the surface the fish are waiting, and, needless to say, many caddis pupae end their lives long before they reach their final destination and become a "fluttering adult."

Good imitations of the pupae are rare, and until recently no attempt had been made to bring them into order in the form of a series of artificials designed specifically to represent the many species of caddis found in America. Nevertheless, anglers successfully overcame the handicap by using traditional wet flies in the same general color and size as those of the migrating pupae with some success, which seems to prove my own theory that many of the wet flies designed by pioneering fly anglers were not meant to imitate a "drowned" mayfly, but rather inconspicuously imitated the pupae.

The length of the fully developed natural pupa ranges from 4mm to 30mm, depending on the species. The pupa's anatomy is much like the adult's, with the exception of the wings. The thorax and abdomen portion is developed distinctly, but the wings, which are contained in the wing cases located on each side of the thorax, are slanted down and project toward the rear, covering portions of the abdomen sides. On top of the head are two long antennae that appear to be fully developed, and the legs are clearly visible and slanted back past the posterior end of the abdomen. For the purpose of fishing, it would be a foolish and time-consuming job to make an imitative copy of each of the many hundreds of pupae in existence, so I have used Eric Leiser's "size and color" approach in designing my pupa imitations, which means that a few flies in several colors and many sizes will cover the needs for fishing anywhere in the country.

The biggest problem in imitating the naturals is to incorporate the glistering sheen of the silvery air bubbles trapped within the translucent pupal skin. When the seal was added to the list of endangered species there were a few moments of panic. Now there is Seal-Ex and SLF, a seal-fur substitute that is available from your material supplier. It is rich in sheen and translucency and lends itself magnificently to the pupa dressings. Because of its coarseness, Seal-Ex can be mixed with some rabbit or mink fur of the same color for dressing the smaller sizes without sacrificing its effectiveness.

When fishing the pupa, one must try to imitate its natural movements and rise to the surface. This is best done by casting it upstream and letting it sink down before applying rhythmic movements with the rod tip and giving a swimming motion to the artificial as it works its way up. To hasten the sink rate, I often apply some windings of .010 lead wire on the hook shank before it is dressed.

For the tying instructions I have chosen a dark brown caddis pupa dressed on a Mustad 3906, size 10. The dark brown is the representative for a number of important artificials that can be fished in both Eastern and Western streams. When dressed in different sizes they will match most of the dark-brown naturals found in the area being fished. If in doubt about which color pupa to use, I collect and open some caddis cases that are closed on both ends, which means that pupation is in progress, and thus determine the color and size found in a particular stream. Like the caddis larva, the pupa is fairly easy to dress, and I often use my streamside tying kit right on the spot if additional flies are needed.

Dark Brown Caddis Pupa

Body Length	9 to 17mm
Representing	Grannom (size 10 to 14),
	Dark Blue Sedge (size 10 to 14),
	Dark Brown Sedge (size 6 to 8)
Availability	The dark-brown variety of caddis pupa are

found in both Eastern and Western streams, and I have had some very fine fishing particularly in Northeastern streams with both the Grannom and the Dark Blue Sedge. It seems that the fish will take this type of artificial more readily when some motion is generated to the fly with erratic movements of the rod tip. Even dragging it in the surface film has stirred up some violent strikes.

Hook	Mustad 3906, size 6 to 14
Thread	Brown, prewaxed 6/0
Abdomen	Dark-brown Seal-Ex or SLF dubbing,
	or latex dyed dark brown
Wing Cases	Two gray rooster or hen body
	feathers trimmed to shape
Thorax and Legs	Well-marked guard hairs and fur from the
	back of brown rabbit dyed dark brown
Head	Brown tying thread
Dubbing Formula	No mixing
Tinting	None

1. Attach the tying thread in front and wind it to a position midway down the hook bend. (If additional weight is desired, it should be added now by winding some .010 lead wire on the shank and covering it with tying thread.) Now form a 3-inch spinning loop using your dubbing wheel and insert a moderate amount of dubbing.

3. Apply a small amount of clear cement on the hook shank and wind the dubbing forward with close turns to a position one-fourth of a body length from the eye. Secure the dubbing tightly with tying thread at that point and trim away the surplus. Now trim the body portion lightly with your scissors, removing uneven spots and stray fibers.

2. Spin a tapered "fur rope." It should be spun tightly enough to create a segmented effect when wound on, and be heavy enough to produce an abdomen of the proportion seen in the finished fly.

4. Select two gray body feathers and remove the soft fibers and fuzz at the base.

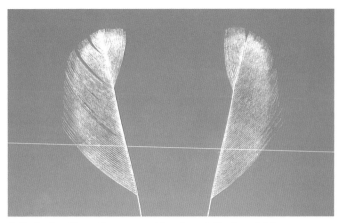

5. Strip the fibers from one side of each feather. Make sure you strip them as seen in the photo so you can make a left and a right wing.

7. Tie in a wing section on each side of the body and form a 3-inch (75mm) spinning loop directly in front of the wings for making the leg section. The procedure for making the fur leg section is explained in Chapter 3 (Tying the Mayfly Nymph) steps 7, 8, 9, and 10.

6. Stroke down a few fibers in reverse and set them in cement. This will make them easy to set when tying them in. Next, cut the feathers to length. They should be long enough to reach down to two thirds body length. Now trim them to the shape as seen in the photo, using the method explained Chapter 4 for making the cut-wings, steps 2, 3, and 4.

8. Apply a little cement on the hook shank, then wind the fur in front of the abdomen and trim the top and sides a little, but leave the underside long to represent the legs. Wind a small head before applying the head cement and the pupa is finished. To make the pupa a little more durable, I sometimes smear a little cement on top of the thorax and sides.

The Latex Pupa

While I use the latex body primarily for the caddis larva, it does make a very attractive abdomen for the larger pupa, although it lacks somewhat the fine translucency of Seal-Ex and SLF.

1. Tie in a strip of latex wide enough for the size pupa being dressed, in this case a size 10, for which the latex strip should be about $1/8$-inch wide. When it is tied in midway down the bend of the hook, the additional weight should be applied if needed. To build up the body I use a fine strand of crewel wool of the same color as the finished abdomen. Be careful not to make the underbody too bulky; remember the latex will be wound over.

2. Then wind the latex strip forward over the underbody with very little stretch. It should be wound in such a way that each turn overlaps the previous one by half its width in order to get a nice segmented effect. Tie off the latex in front about one-fourth of a body length from the eye and cut the surplus.

3. The rest of the pupa is now finished in the same manner as described in the tying instructions for the dark brown caddis pupa. To get the color abdomen called for in the various dressings, the latex strips can either be dyed or tinted with Pantone markers.

Selected Pupa Dressings

Note: While all the dressings call for guard hair and fur from the back of a brown rabbit that has been dyed to give it a uniform color and darken the lighter guard hairs, this is not to say that other types of animals with the same characteristics cannot be used, or even be necessary, particularly in the smaller sizes. The Australian opossum is good for pupa dressings, as is the hare's mask. In any case, good judgment in selecting a substitute is needed to achieve the effect of the rabbit.

Medium Brown Pupa

Body Length	6 to 16mm
Representing	Medium Brown Sedge (size 8 to 10), Little Brown Sedge (size 14 to 16)
Availability	The medium brown pupa is useful for fishing in Eastern and Western streams alike. For some reason I never fail to get a few fish on a size 10 Medium Brown very early in the season. Since most streams are high and fairly fast at that time, I wind some .010 lead wire on the hook shank for extra weight before the body is applied.

Hook	Mustad 3906, size 8 to 16
Thread	Brown, prewaxed 6/0
Abdomen	Medium-brown Seal-Ex or SLF dubbing, or latex strip dyed medium brown
Wing Cases	Two gray rooster or hen body feathers trimmed to shape
Thorax and Legs	Well-marked guard hairs and fur from the back of a brown rabbit dyed brown
Head	Brown tying thread
Dubbing Formula	No mixing
Tinting	None

Pale Brown Pupa

Body Length	9 to 13mm
Representing	Spotted Sedge (size 14), Speckled Sedge (size 10)
Availability	Like most other caddis, the Pale Brown is found in both Eastern and Western rivers, and the artificials are effective most any time of the year, although late spring and early summer seem to be the time when they hatch. Try to fish it in the shallows late in the day or early evening by imitating the swimming movements so characteristic of the caddis pupa.

Hook	Mustad 3906, size 10 to 14
Thread	Brown, prewaxed 6/0
Abdomen	Pale-brown Seal-Ex dubbing, or latex strip dyed pale brown
Wing Cases	Two gray rooster or hen body feathers trimmed to shape
Thorax and Legs	Well-marked guard hairs and fur from the back of a brown rabbit dyed brown
Head	Brown tying thread
Dubbing Formula	3 parts buff and1 part medium brown
Tinting	The pale brown is not easy to dye, so if latex is used for the abdomen, it is better to tint it pale brown with a Pantone 162M. The marker looks pink, but when applied generously it dries pale brown on latex.

Gray Caddis Pupa

Body Length   6 to 13mm
Representing   Several gray and brownish-gray species
Availability   The gray pupa I carry in my fly box is a general representative of a number of caddis of that color, and I believe they will work anywhere in the country, although I have never found it to be as effective as the brown variety.

Hook	Mustad 3906, size 10 to 16
Thread	Brown, prewaxed 6/0
Abdomen	Grayish-brown Seal-Ex, SLF or latex strip
Wing Cases	Two gray rooster or hen body feathers trimmed to shape
Thorax and legs	Well-marked guard hairs and fur from the back of a brown rabbit dyed brown
Head	Brown tying thread
Dubbing Formula	2 parts medium gray and 1 part medium brown
Tinting	If latex is used, it should be tinted with a light-gray Pantone 413M

Cinnamon Sedge

Body Length   13 to 16mm
Representing   Cinnamon Sedge
Availability   My experience with the Cinnamon Pupa has been on Northeastern streams in late summer, but I see no reason why it should not be effective in other parts of the country.

Hook	Mustad 3906, size 8 to 10
Thread	Brown, prewaxed 6/0
Abdomen	Orangish-brown Seal-Ex or SLF dubbing, or latex strip
Wing Cases	Two gray rooster or hen body feathers trimmed to shape
Thorax and Legs	Well-marked guard hairs and fur from the back of a brown rabbit dyed dark brown
Head	Brown tying thread
Dubbing Formula	3 parts medium brown, 1 part burnt orange, and 1 part yellowish-orange
Tinting	If latex is used, it is first tinted with a yellowish-orange Pantone 150M, then with a brown 154M; the brown should be dabbed on lightly

American Sand Sedge

Body Length   9 to 13mm
Representing   Sand Sedge
Availability   This pupa can be productive both in Eastern and Western streams and is active from late winter through early summer, depending on the location being fished.

Hook   Mustad 3906, size 10 to 14
Thread   Brown, prewaxed 6/0
Abdomen   Dirty-yellow Seal-Ex or SLF dubbing, or latex strip
Wing Cases   Two gray rooster or hen body feathers trimmed to shape
Thorax and Legs   Well-marked guard hairs and fur from the back of a brown rabbit dyed brown
Head   Brown tying thread
Dubbing Formula   Yellow Seal-Ex until it appears as a dirty-yellow dubbing
Tinting   A latex abdomen should first be tinted yellow with a Pantone 115M, then with a gray Pantone 413M; it is given a light touch-up to produce the dirty-yellow appearance

Bright Green Pupa

Body Length   13 to 16mm
Representing   Western Caperer (size 8 to 10), Dark Olive Sedge (size 8 to 10)
Availability   The subsurface stage of the Bright Green variety has been popular among serious fly fishers for as long as I can remember, and whether you fish Eastern or Western streams, this is one pattern that should not be left out.

Hook   Mustad 3906, size 8 to 10
Thread   Brown, prewaxed 6/0
Abdomen   Bright-grass-green Seal-Ex or SLF dubbing touched up lightly on the back with black marking pen, or latex strip dyed bright green
Wing Cases   Two gray rooster or hen body feathers trimmed to shape
Thorax and Legs   Well-marked guard hairs and fur from the back of a brown rabbit dyed brown
Head   Brown tying thread
Dubbing Formula   No mixing
Tinting   The abdomen on pupae dressed with either Seal-Ex or SLF dubbing or latex should be touched up lightly on the back with a black marker; if this seems too dark, use a very dark green

Pale Olive Pupa

Body Length	9 to 13mm
Representing	Olive Sedges
Availability	Like the larger Bright Green Pupa, the Olives are favorites in the East and West both, where they represent a number of different species of caddis that are of importance to the angler.

Hook	Mustad 3906, size 10 to 14
Thread	Brown, prewaxed 6/0
Abdomen	Pale-olive Seal-Ex dubbing or SLF or latex strip
Wing Cases	Two gray rooster or hen body feathers trimmed to shape
Thorax and Legs	Well-marked guard hairs and fur from the back of a brown rabbit dyed brown
Head	Brown tying thread
Dubbing Formula	2 parts medium olive and 1 part yellow
Tinting	A latex abdomen should be tinted with a yellowish-olive Pantone 104M

Large Reddish-Brown Pupa

Body Length	17 to 21mm
Representing	Large Red Sedge
Availability	The Reddish-Brown Pupa is among the largest of the caddis found in America and I believe it can be fished successfully anywhere in the country. Its large size should be particularly interesting for those who go after big fish at night.

Hook	Mustad 3906, size 4 to 6
Thread	Brown, prewaxed 6/0
Abdomen	Dark reddish-brown Seal-Ex or SLF dubbing, or latex strip dyed dark reddish-brown
Wing Cases	Two gray rooster or hen body feathers trimmed to shape
Thorax and Legs	Well-marked guard hairs and fur from the back of a brown rabbit dyed dark brown
Head	Brown tying thread
Dubbing Formula	2 parts dark brown and 1 part reddish-brown
Tinting	None

Caddis Pupae of Minute Sizes

There are times when the fish will start to feed on the tiniest members of the caddis family, some of them so small that it is impractical even to attempt to make a copy; it would appear as a mere speck. In later years, however, it has become fashionable to fish minute-sized artificials with midge rods and delicate 7X or 8X tippets. Most of the dressings of the larger pupae can be made up on smaller hook sizes such as 18, 20, and 22, with just a few changes in the material list. Narrow strips of latex are excellent for these tiny sizes, whereas the Seal-Ex dubbing must be substituted with a softer fur such as mink. The wing cases are completely omitted, but the thorax and leg method of dressing is retained, provided that some suitable guard-hair fur, such as hare's or Australian opossum mask, can be obtained. If this type of material is not on hand, they can be dressed by tying a few fibers under the body as a beard and a dark-brown fur thorax applied in front, using the same roll dubbing method as for a dry fly.

DRESSING THE CADDIS ADULT, STEP BY STEP

Except perhaps in some European countries, the caddisflies, or sedges as they are often called, have not been considered of major interest to the angler except in their subaquatic form. As a dry fly, their existence was somewhat overshadowed by flies of the major hatches. But a few years ago they suddenly accelerated in popularity and now demand equal space in our dry-fly boxes. Very often, I am sure, some of the traditional dries like the Light Cahill, Quill Gordon, and Adams have taken trout that somehow mistook them for being caddisflies, which doesn't make sense at all since trout are supposed to be selective and know the difference.

There are two types that have proved their worth. Both were designed by Larry Solomon of New York City, whose skill as an angler-writer is matched only by his innovative methods at the vise. Larry has spent a great deal of time in his research, studying the behavior pattern and availability of many of the most common caddis of interest to the angler. The first pattern is a hair-wing artificial; the wing consists of a bunch of deer body hair dressed as a down-wing, lying very low and parallel with the fur body. The tips of the wings extend beyond the hook bend and aid the fly in floating much like the tail on the traditional dry fly. The floating hackle is applied in the conventional dry-fly manner after the wing has been secured. Larry designed the hair-wing caddis to imitate the emerged adult and considers it as his standard caddis dry-fly imitation.

The second design is a delta-wing pattern; the deer-hair wing is replaced by hackle points tied on either side of the body in a jetlike manner. The specific intention of the delta-wing was to imitate a caddis that, for one reason or another, found itself in a disabled condition after emerging, unable to take off and an easy target for the trout, which will feed on such unfortunate insects in a very leisurely manner, completely contrary to their normal splashy approach.

Adult caddisflies, or sedges, look very much like moths and they are closely related. Their wings are rather long in relation to their relatively short body, and in comparison with the mayfly adult, seem completely out of proportion. When the insect is at rest the wings are folded and lie down over the body in the tentlike manner characteristic of most mothlike insects. The wings are rather hairy, a condition which undoubtedly prompted the entomologists to classify the caddis insects as Trichoptera (*trichos* = hair, and *pteron* = wing), which is coincidental to the fact that the artificial flies are called hair-winged caddis.

The two long antennae located on the forehead of the insect are omitted on the artificial as they have no bearing on effectiveness. Like most other insects, the caddis has six legs located on the thorax portion. The two rear legs are almost covered by the straddling wings when the caddis is at rest. The color of these insects varies according to species, and I suggest that you collect some specimens of the naturals on the stream being fished. During a heavy caddis hatch there may be several species of different colors intermixed. The trout are often selective, feeding only on one particular insect and ignoring the rest. Their peculiar behavior, dancing or fluttering about on or near the surface film, can be observed by kneeling down and focusing your attention on the water surface against the light. A small aquarium net is usually large enough to capture some specimens for closer examination.

The dressing procedure is quite simple, but until you have mastered the various manipulations, I suggest you use a Mustad 94833, 3X Super Fine Wire, size 10. The color combination used for the instructions is incidental and may be changed to suit an individual taste.

Hair-Wing Caddis

Common Name	Hair-Wing caddis with specific color named in front
Order	Tricoptera
Genus and Species	Various
Availability	Found on most streams and lakes

throughout the country from April through late September depending on the species. The heaviest concentration occurs in late afternoon and early evening and good days can often generate blizzardlike hatches.

Hook	Mustad 94833, size 10 to 22
Thread	Brown, prewaxed 6/0
Body	Dark-olive fur dubbing
Wings	Medium-brown hackle tips or deer body hair
Hackle	Medium-brown rooster hackle
Head	Brown tying thread

1. Attach the tying thread in front and wrap the entire shank of the hook with thread to a position shown, then roll the fur dubbing on the tying thread.

2. Wind the dubbing on the hook shank in the same manner as for a traditional dry-fly body so that it covers two-thirds of the shank. Tie off the dubbing and cut the surplus, then wind some tying thread in front of the dubbed body, building up a level foundation for the wing, which will otherwise sit too high when tied in.

3. Cut a large bunch of hair close to the skin and remove the underfur.

5. Place the hair on top of the hook with the tips extending a full body length beyond the hook bend. Take a couple of loose thread windings to hold them in place, then roll the hair down a little on each side of the shank and tighten them securely in that position. Trim the butt ends and apply a little clear cement. Make sure the wing is sitting flat and unflared.

4. Align the hair in a stacker. Insert the hair tips first, as shown. Shake the container, and the hair aligns itself.

6. Tie in two dry-fly hackles selected properly for the hook size desired. They are tied in at the same time with the dull undersides together.

An adult delta-wing caddis. The tying method for this caddis is the same as that for the previous pattern, except for the wings.

The Delta-Wing Dressing for the Caddis Adult

The dressing procedures for this artificial are identical to that for the hair-wing, with the obvious exception of the wing.

Delta-Wing Caddis

Hook	Mustad 94833, size 10 to 22
Thread	Brown, prewaxed 6/0
Body	Dark-olive fur dubbing
Wings	Medium-brown hackle tips or deer body hair
Hackle	Medium-brown rooster hackle
Head	Brown tying thread

7. Wind the hackles one at a time in traditional dry-fly style and wind a small head in front before finishing the fly with a little clear cement on the thread windings.

1. Complete Steps 1 and 2 of the instructions for the hair-wing, then select two hackle tips of the proper color (in this case, medium brown) and tie them on in front on each side of the body so that they stand out at a 45-degree angle. The wings should be long enough to extend slightly beyond the hook bend. A properly set wing should be parallel with or slightly below the top of the body.

2. Attach and wind the hackles in the same manner as for the hair-wing, and the delta-wing caddis is finished.

Body and Hackle Variation

An interesting method of body dressing and hackle trimming was shown to me by Walt Dette, the celebrated Catskill fly dresser whose creations of fur and feather have set a standard for many a traditional fly pattern. He uses leftover hackle which he trims so that only the small stumps of barbules are left on the stem, then winds it on the hook shank with close turns laid side by side. This makes for a very translucent and extremely durable body and puts into use the less desirable hackles that always clutter the tying bench.

Dette's trimmed-hackle body ready for use with either a hair-wing or delta-wing caddis is shown above.

3. The finished Delta-Wing Caddis.

When Walt has finished his fly he likes it to sit very low on the water in a fashion characteristic of the natural insect, and here is where he breaks the unwritten rule of fly tying. He trims the floating hackle. When reminded of his sin, he grins and makes reference to those artificials with no hackle at all. The hackle trimming is very specific and done with great care so that it will not ruin the balance or overall attractiveness of the fly. It is trimmed across underneath the body so the hackle fibers are of a length equal to the hook gap. This leaves the fibers on the side upon which the fly will float full length. A front view of Dette's trimmed floating hackle is shown above.

Additional Patterns for Adult Caddis

There are many hundreds of adult caddis varieties, which differ in both size and color. I suggest that you collect some specimens from the water you are fishing and make notes about size and color for reference when you're dressing your flies.

Caddisflies swarming over long grass. Soon the trout will start feeding. Photo by Michael Jensen

Chapter 6
Stonefly Nymphs

The nymph of the adult stonefly is one of the most effective artificials I have ever used on a trout stream. Much like the pupa and larva of our caddisflies, they can be fished throughout the season anywhere in the country. I do not mean to imply that the species of a particular genus does not have a certain time of hatching, but their long growth period (as long as three years) makes them more available and they are ever present, crawling among rocks in the streambeds of swift rivers where sufficient oxygen can be generated for their existence. When they are ready to hatch they migrate to shallow areas and crawl up on rocks or debris; there their skin splits open and the adult insect appears. The hatching usually takes place very early in the morning. If you are walking along the rocky shores of a stream and you notice the empty skins on the stones it is an indication that a hatch is in progress or has just taken place.
At such times you can pick an artificial that closely matches the skins in size and color and often have some spectacular fishing, particularly if you get to the stream before daybreak.

The structural appearances of all stonefly nymphs are almost identical, so for the purpose of dressing the artificials they will be treated as such. The few minor differences that might be present from pattern to pattern will be explained in specific dressings.

Stoneflies are generally flat throughout and have a long segmented abdomen with two tails at the posterior end. They are easily distinguished from other nymphs because they have two beautifully marked wing cases; the mayfly nymph has only one. They are located on the thorax portion, which represents the front half of the nymph. The head is quite large and flat with two antennae that are about half as long as the tails. The six legs are rather strong in appearance and have a small claw on the end, which makes them ideally suited for a nymph that lives among rocks and debris on the stream bottom. The body of a mature nymph, excluding tails and antennae, is about 6mm to 5mm (¼-inch to 2 inches) and ranges in color from pale yellow, amber, and tan to brown and black. In most cases the bottom portion of the nymph is much lighter than the top, if not entirely different. Those who care to collect some specimens

for use as models will find that the empty skins found along the stream will do nicely, but they are pretty fragile. Live insects can be collected from the streambed by placing a large piece of screening or net downstream from the place you are searching, then roughing up the stream bottom and turning over stone and debris. The dislodged insects are carried into the collecting net by the current, after which they can be picked up and placed in suitable containers.

When you find the nymphal skin of a stonefly on a rock by the river, select an artificial close to its size and color.

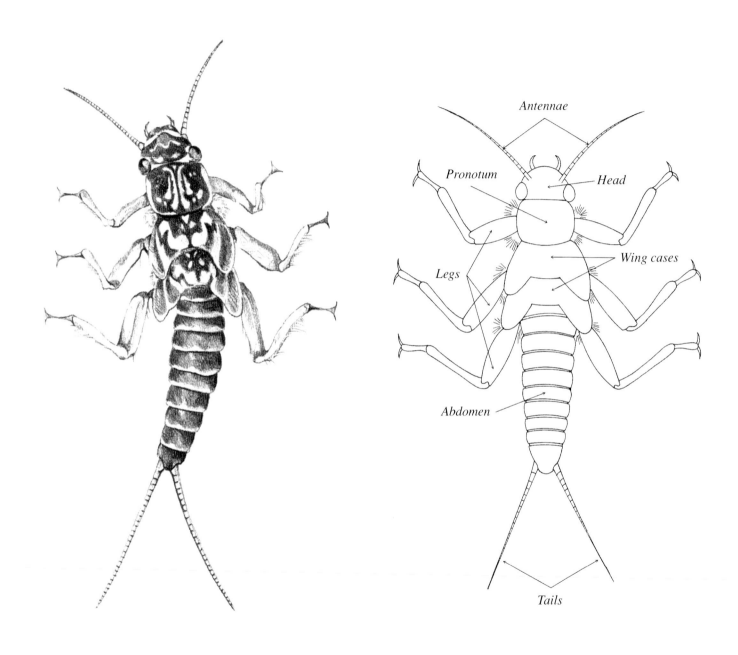

Stonefly nymph   Anatomy of a stonefly nymph

DRESSING THE STONEFLY NYMPH, STEP BY STEP

The nymph I am using as a model for the dressing instructions is a well-known Eastern species: *Perla capitata,* better known as the *Perla* Stonefly Creeper in the East. The specimen I am copying was collected on the Beaverkill in the Catskills in the month of August, where the rocks in the shallows of School-house Pool were cluttered with nymphal shucks, and adult stoneflies appeared everywhere along the banks in the early morning hours. Although the nymph can be fished throughout the season, my notes indicate that I have taken more fish on this particular artificial during the summer months. Unlike some of the large Western stoneflies, *Perla* is rarely of any value in its adult stage dressed as a dry fly, and I don't carry any in my fly box.

The first and foremost consideration before starting to copy any specific insect is to evaluate its dimension, and this is perhaps more important for stoneflies than for any other insects because of their unique structure. Aside from having two distinct wing cases, there is one more important factor that makes them different from other nymphs and larvae: they have a smooth outer shell without hairy filaments, as opposed to the mayfly nymph with its breathing gills along either side of the abdomen. When dressing stoneflies, I strongly urge that you closely follow the proportions prescribed and shown in the drawing, or the end result, regardless of your fly-tying skill, will be an absolute disaster.

Perla Stonefly Creeper

Body Length	15 to 28mm
Hook	Partridge CS10, Bartleet salmon hook size 6 or 8, or Mustad 38941 3X Long, size 6–10
Thread	Yellow, 6/0
Underbody	Lead wire (.025 inches) wound on middle $^1/_3$ of hook shank
Tails	Two goose biots dyed tan, $^1/_3$ body length
Body and Ribbing	Tan Seal-Ex or SLF dubbing rear $^2/_3$ of body, ribbed with thin brown Larva Lace or heavy tying thread
Wing Cases	Two folds of tan Swiss straw
Legs	Well-marked guard hair with underfur from the back of a brown rabbit spun in a loop
Antennae	Tan goose biots, half as long as tails (optional)
Head	Tying thread and small remainder of front wing case

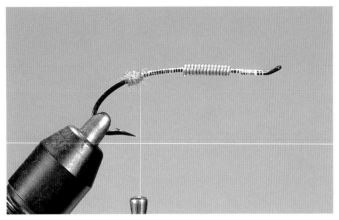

1. Cover the hook shank with tying thread, then roll a very small amount of dubbing on the thread and form a small ball directly above the hook barb. Now wind some .025-inch lead wire on the middle $1/3$ of the hook shank.

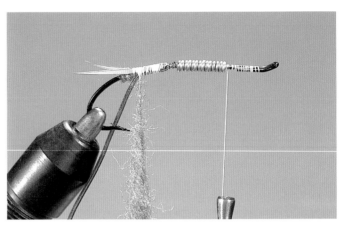

3. Tie in the ribbing directly in front of the fur ball. Make a 3-inch spinning loop, insert the body material and spin a rope-like dubbing. It should be quite heavy but not wound too tight so it will create a segmented body.

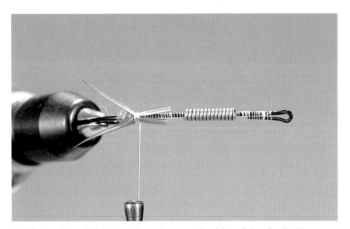

2. Tie in the tail biots splayed on each side of the fur ball as seen. They should be as long as $1/3$ body length.

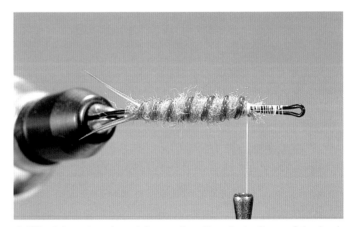

4. Wind the tying thread forward to directly in front of the lead wire segment and let it hang. Now wind the dubbing forward over the shank and tie it off. Spiral the ribbing over the body and tie it off. Trim the surplus material and let the tying thread hang at the tie-off spot ready for the wing material to be tied in.

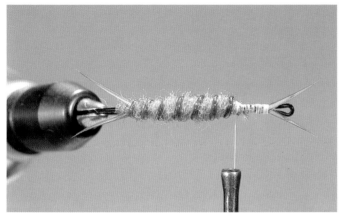

5. If you want the fly to have antennae, you should tie them in now as shown. They are ¹/₅ the body length long.

7. Place your dubbing needle at a position ¹/₃ of the dubbed body length from the front of the body. Double the wing material over the needle and tie it down in front of the body. This completes the first wing case.

6. Select a 3-inch (75mm) length of Swiss straw and carefully unravel it. Give it a light coat of tying cement and refold it so it's a little wider than the front of the body. If not cemented, it will widen when wet. Now tie it in flat in front of the body, with the long end projecting toward the rear.

8. Pull the remainder of the wing case material back over the body to the rear and tie it down in front of the first wing case, then form a 1¹/₂-inch-long spinning loop and form the leg section as explained in steps 6, 7, and 8 for the caddis pupa in Chapter 5. The fur in the loop should be long enough to reach to the middle of the body when wound on the hook.

9. Wind the fur leg section in front of the wing case and tie it off close to the eye. Separate the fur on top and pull it down to each side of the body. Your fly should now be as shown in the photo.

11. Side view of the finished nymph.

10. Place your dubbing needle on the wing case material at a point even with the middle of the first wing case. Fold the material forward over the needle and tie it down in front of the fur leg section. Add some additional thread windings and tie off with a whip finish. Trim the surplus wing case material but leave a small amount to represent the head.

Note On Additional Patterns

Since there are so many different species of stoneflies throughout the world, I suggest that you examine the water in the area where you are fishing, collect some samples, and study the color and size for selection of hook and material. With that information you can tie any stonefly nymph you find by using the tying instruction for the Perla Stonefly Creeper.

THE ADULT STONEFLY

Stonefly nymphs are undoubtedly the most important to the fish and the angler, but one should not underestimate the importance of the winged adults. In the western United States and other places in the world, they are of great importance. My notes tell me that they appear all through the fishing season. Since there are many different species in both size and color, it's best to collect a few samples from the area where you are fishing.

Coastal Deer Hair Stonefly (simple)

Hook	Mustad 80050BR, size 6 to 14
Thread	Tan, prewaxed 6/0
Body	Coastal deer body hair, spun and trimmed
Ribbing	Tan tying thread
Thorax	Hare's mask dubbing, dyed black
Wings	Two blue dun hackle tips set flat over body
Head	Tan tying thread

Coastal Deer Hair Stonefly (realistic)

Hook	Mustad 80050BR, size 6 to 14
Thread	Tan, prewaxed 6/0
Body	Coastal deer hair, spun and trimmed
Ribbing	Tan tying thread
Thorax	Hare's mask dubbing, dyed black
Wings	Two back feathers from a golden pheasant, dyed gray, with fibers reversed and set in tying cement
Head	Tan tying thread

Note the flat look of this adult stonefly. This shape is what the patterns above are supposed to imitate. PHOTO BY MORTEN VALEUR

Chapter 7
Hellgrammite Larvae
and Crustaceans

I have often wondered if many of the well-known Woolly Worms were not meant to imitate the hellgrammite and other similar-looking creatures such as the fish fly larvae and others found throughout the country. My own personal experience with the hellgrammite comes from the Potomac River in Maryland, where they are in great abundance, and consequently imitations have become very popular among those who fish for smallmouth bass. Great many anglers will search the rocky bottom of the swiftest part of the river for the larvae and use them as live bait wherever it is legal. I have used a number of good imitations for smallmouth bass on that river with good success, but they work equally well on a trout stream early in the season or for night fishing when the big fish are on the prowl. Since their natural habitat is among rocks on the stream bottom, the artificials should be weighted to keep them down deep in the faster water.

Being the larval stage of the large dobsonfly, the hellgrammite reaches an enormous size at maturity, and specimens 2 to 3 inches long are not uncommon, although artificials are rarely dressed any larger than 1 1/2 to 2 inches at the most. It is a vicious looking creature, predominantly flat and blackish-brown throughout its entire length. The six legs are blackish-brown and rather short in relation to the total length of the larva. The abdomen portion has lateral appendages of a dark-brownish color at each segment on either side, which in fly tying are referred to as gills. The top of the thorax has a hard, shiny, blackish-brown shell or wing case that is almost square, and in front of the head are two heavy mandibles capable of pinching the collector's finger. If you collect hellgrammite larva for models in fly tying, I recommend that you use a net or a seine. When they are captured they can be grasped on top of the hard-shelled wing case and placed in a suitable container.

Hellgrammite Larva

Body Length	25 to 35mm
Hook	Partridge Traditional Bartleet Salmon, CS10/1, size 2 or 4
Thread	Black, prewaxed 6/0
Tail	A small bunch of dyed dark-brown cock pheasant tail fiber tips, very short
Underbody	A piece of .032 lead wire secured on each side of the hook shank with tying thread and clear cement
Body	Equal parts of black and dark-brown Seal-Ex or SLF dubbing, ribbed with medium-wide brown latex to form the segments
Gills	One black and one dark-brown saddle hackle palmered wet-fly style, following front of ribbing and trimmed away top and bottom; sides trimmed to gill length
Thorax and Wing Shell	Blackish-brown dyed rabbit fur from the back with heavy guard hairs unblended from the skin, spun in a loop and wound as a wet-fly hackle; black-and-brown-mottled turkey tail strip tied over and set in clear cement to form wing shell
Mandibles	Two fibers left from excess wing-shell material
Legs	Fur and guard hairs from thorax left as is or shaped into three legs on each side with clear cement

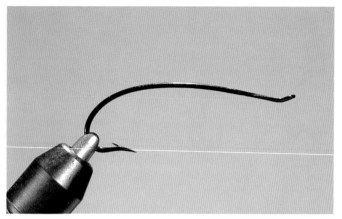

forming the underbody will give the finished body a flat effect in addition to the added weight needed when a nymph or larva must be fished deep. If no weight is needed, the body should still be flat, and the lead wire strips are replaced by two pieces of monofilament of the same diameter and attached to the shank in the same manner as described for the lead. If medium weight is needed after adding the monofilament, you can wind some .010 lead wire on a portion of the underbody and cover it with thread before the overbody is applied.

1. Since the body of this larva is not natural-looking if dressed on a straight hook, I start the fly by forming the shank of the desired-size hook to a slight arc and opening the hook gap a little with a pair of needlenose pliers

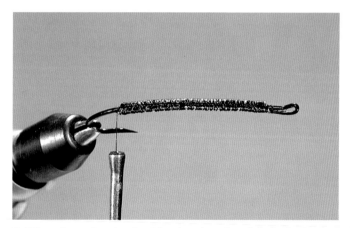

2. Wrap the entire shank with tying thread and tie in the lead wire on each side of the hook shank. The lead should be fastened tightly and kept directly alongside the shank. Use your needlenose pliers across the wire and the shank to make it even on both sides. Cover the lead wire completely with tying thread and apply some clear cement on the windings. This method of

3. Take the tying thread to the shank portion directly to the rear of the underbody and tie in four to six dark-brown fiber tips. Trim away the surplus butt ends and advance the tying thread to directly on the rearmost part of the underbody and tie in a 6-inch length of black raffia or latex on top for ribbing.

4. Prepare the gill hackles to be tied in wet-fly style. This is done by stroking the hackles down the center spine until the fibers stand out at a right angle. Now cut away the tip portions and trim the fibers on both sides about $1/2$-inch up the stem, leaving only small stumps so they won't slip when tied in.

6. Form a 4-inch spinning loop at the position where the hackles and ribbing are tied in and spin a fairly heavy dubbing mixture.

5. Tie in the hackles in the same position as the ribbing, making sure that each is securely fastened and that there is a small portion of bare stem between the first fibers and the tie-in point. This makes it easier to start the hackle when winding it.

7. Hold the hackles and ribbing straight up and apply a small amount of clear cement on the underbody. Now take the first turn of dubbing closely behind the two materials, then continue to wind it tightly forward to one-third of a body length from the hook eye and tie it off. Cut the surplus dubbing and spiral the ribbing forward over the dubbed body and tie off in front.

8. Wind the two hackles simultaneously in wet-fly fashion, doubling the fibers back before each turn and following in front of each turn of ribbing. Tie hackles off securely in front and cut away the surplus.

10. For the wing-case shell, prepare a section of black-and-brown-mottled turkey tail that is cut wide enough to be the width of the body when doubled lengthwise. After doubling it, brush it with tying cement and let it dry.

9. Trim away all the fibers close on top and bottom. Then trim the fibers on both sides to approximately one body width, to represent the gills.

11. Tie in the wing-shell material directly in front of the finished abdomen so that it lies flat with the butt ends projecting toward the rear, then secure it tightly on the thorax portion of the underbody. Cut the surplus ends short of the eye and take the tying thread back to directly in front of the abdomen and form a 3-inch spinning loop.

12. Cut a good bunch of fur and guard hairs that are long enough to reach the middle of the body and form the leg section, as explained in the mayfly nymph steps 7–10.

14. The finished hellgrammite larva is now given a good coat of clear lacquer, and while still wet give it a flatter appearance by using your needlenose pliers on the abdomen portion only. Keep applying clear lacquer on the wing shell until it dries with a high shine, and your fly is finished.

13. Divide the fur and guard hairs on top of the thorax and press it down on each side, then apply a small amount of clear cement in the center on top. Grasp the wing-shell material and pull it forward over the fur thorax and tie it down in front. Separate one fiber on each side of the surplus extending forward over the eye and trim away the rest to form the mandibles.

Simplified Hellgrammite and Fish Fly Larva

From a fly fisher's point of view, hellgrammite and fish fly larvae are very much alike in their general appearance, so the Simplified Hellgrammite Larva is for all practical purposes the same as the Simplified Fish Fly Larva or vice versa, except that the Fish Fly is somewhat smaller and has no mandibles.

Hook	Mustad 3665A, 6X Long, size 2 to 6
Thread	Black, prewaxed 6/0
Tail Gills	A small bunch of dyed dark-brown cock pheasant tail fiber tips, very short
Underbody	A piece of .032 lead wire secured on each side of the hook shank with tying thread and clear cement
Body	Dark-brown chenille, medium size
Hackle	Dark-brown saddle hackle palmered, then trimmed top and bottom; remaining fibers on each side trimmed to size for gills

The underbody is formed on the shaped hook in the exact same manner as shown in dressing the Hellgrammite Larva. Tie in the tail gill fibers in the rear, together with the hackle and a 6-inch piece of chenille. Wind the chenille forward on the underbody after applying a coat of clear cement. Go all the way to the front behind the eye with a chenille and tie it off. Cut the surplus and palmer the hackle forward and tie off in front. Trim away the excess hackle and wind a small head. Trim the hackle on the top and bottom and cut the side to the appropriate gill length. To emphasize the flatness, I trim the chenille on the top and bottom a little before applying some clear cement to the whole body, except the gills. When the cement gets a little tacky, I flatten it even more with my needlenose pliers.

CRUSTACEANS

Freshwater shrimp and cress bugs are found in limestone streams and lakes and are an important source of food for fish. Shrimp are in such abundance in some areas that fish pay no attention to hatching mayflies. So if you are fishing a limestone stream or lake where the fish are not rising, it's probably not because there are no fish, but because they're feeding on shrimp.

Cress Bug

Body Length	6 to 12mm
Common Name	Sowbug
Genus	Representative dressing
Availability	Found all year among the elodea in limestone streams.
Hook	Mustad 3906, size 16 to 18
	Mustad 3906B, size 12 to 14
Thread	Olive, prewaxed 6/0
Body	Gray fur with guard hairs dyed medium olive or SLF spun in a loop "chenille style," then wound and trimmed on top, bottom, and sides to a very flat, oval-shaped body
Head	Olive tying thread

Freshwater Shrimp

Body Length	9 to 12mm
Common Name	Yellow scud
Genus	Representative dressing
Availability	Same as cress bug above.

Hook	Mustad 3906B, size 10 to 16
Thread	Olive, prewaxed 6/0
Body	Yellowish-olive dyed fur with guard hairs or SLF spun in a loop "chenille style," then wound and trimmed on top and both sides, leaving the fur and guard hairs long on the underside to represent the legs
Head	Olive tying thread

Selected Patterns

Peacock Shrimp

Hook	Mustad 80250BR, size 8 to 12
Thread	Olive, prewaxed 6/0
Tail	Olive hackle fibers
Body	Olive-brown dubbing
Ribbing	Fine oval gold tinsel
Hackle	Soft hackle, dyed olive, palmered over body
Back	Peacock herl
Head	Olive tying thread

Marabou Shrimp

Hook	Mustad 80250BR, size 12 to 20
Thread	Olive, prewaxed 6/0
Tail	Marabou, dyed olive
Body	Olive marabou, wound like a body
Ribbing	Fine oval golden tinsel
Back	Raffia, dyed olive
Head	Olive tying thread

Egg Sack Shrimp

Hook	Mustad 80200BR, size 8 to 20
Thread	Tan, prewaxed 6/0
Body	Tan mohair, SLF or Seal-Ex dubbing
Ribbing	Fine clear tying thread
Egg Sack	Yellow body dubbing in middle of body
Back	A few strands of peacock herl, lacquered

Note: Pick out the dubbing below to imitate legs, and stroke back above with a little cement on your fingers to form the back.

Gray Shrimp

Hook	Mustad 80200BR, size 8 to 20
Thread	Tan, prewaxed 6/0
Tail	Natural gray mini ostrich herl
Body	Gray mohair, SLF, or Seal-Ex dubbing
Ribbing	Fine clear tying thread
Legs	Natural gray ostrich herl
Back	Lacquer

Note: Pick out the dubbing below to imitate legs, and stroke back above with a little cement on your fingers to form the back.

Opposite: *Kenneth Bostrom and Preben Torp Jacobsen fish the Letort Spring Creek in Pennsylvania.*

Chapter 8
Terrestrial Insects

As far as I can determine, there is little doubt that terrestrial fishing emanated on the Pennsylvania limestone streams near Carlisle, where Vince Marinaro and Charles K. Fox, two of America's most distinguished anglers, refined to a science the methods of angling with hoppers, crickets, beetles, and ants, aided by their tobacco-chewing friend Ross Trimmer, whose ability with rod and vise was overshadowed only by his ability to talk louder and laugh harder than anyone else. By sharing their experiences they laid the foundation of a new era of dry-fly fishing, which has been built upon enthusiastically by others. We are grateful to them not only for the opportunity of an extended dry-fly season, but also for giving the fly tier an excuse to work overtime at the vise.

BEETLES (COLEOPTERA)

On some trout streams, and it doesn't much matter where in the country, there is no artificial fly that works better than a small beetle, particularly a black one. On windy days they are often blown into the water and find themselves struggling on the surface for survival, but few manage to reach shore before falling prey to a hungry trout.

My favorite is one made from deer body hair that has been dyed black, although there are times when one dressed with natural dun-gray works well. I once met a delightful fellow on the stream who tied all his deer-hair beetles in white and carried waterproof marking pens of various colors in his vest so that he could always "match the beetle hatch" no matter where he happened to be. While the deer-hair beetle is made entirely from one bunch of hair manipulated onto the hook in the form of the natural insect, there is a feather beetle which is more delicate and less bulky, a reason I suspect for choosing it when fishing over native browns in Pennsylvania's slow-moving limestone streams. I am including dressings for both types of beetles, two favorites of mine—though there are undoubtedly others that would work just as well.

From Left: *Black Deer-Hair Beetle, Feather Beetle, Fur Ant.*

Black Deer-Hair Beetle

Hook	Mustad 94833, size 14 to 20
Thread	Black, prewaxed 6/0
Body	Black tying thread over deer body hair
Legs	Surplus hair tips divided and set spentwing style with crisscross windings; trimmed to size of legs after back is finished
Back	Deer body hair pulled forward over body and tied down in front, then set in clear lacquer
Head	Trimmed deer hair butts from back material

Note: You may not care for these types of legs on your beetles, but they are more durable than those made by separating three fibers on each side, as was previously the case. A "six-leg" arrangement can be made by using very thin tinted rubber string such as is often used on bass bugs, or simply heavy sewing thread tied in at the leg position and with the ends lacquered so they won't unravel. This type of leg should be secured on the underside of the body and positioned one-third body length from the hook eye.

1. Wrap the entire hook shank with tying thread to a point past the barb and tie in a bunch of deer body hair with the tips projecting forward over the eye. Secure it very tightly with thread, binding the hair down for two-thirds of the shank. The front third must be clear so the back can be tied down and a head formed. Before proceeding, give the tied-down body portion a good coat of clear lacquer.

3. Grasp the long deer-hair ends that are projecting to the rear and pull them forward over the body, then tie them down on the shank in front. Pull them tight before they are secured completely, and also remove any short hairs that might not have been long enough to start with or have broken in the process.

2. Separate the hair tips into two equal bunches and set them in the position seen with crisscross windings and a little clear cement.

4. Trim the surplus back hair short in front to form the head, and also trim the leg hair to size (one-third body length). Now give the beetle several good coats of clear lacquer on the head and back, as well as underneath, and it is finished.

Black Feather Beetle

Hook	Mustad 94833, size 12 to 20
Thread	Black, prewaxed 6/0
Body	Peacock herl palmered with black rooster hackle, trimmed top and bottom
Wing	Two metallic-colored feathers from collar of ring-neck pheasant lacquered together and trimmed to shape
Head	Black tying thread

2. Wind the herl underbody with close turns and tie it off in front. Cut the surplus and spiral the hackle in palmered-style over it forward to the front. Take a couple of extra turns to represent the legs before tying off and cutting the surplus. Now trim away all the fibers on the underside leaving the top and sides long.

1. Wrap the entire shank with tying thread and tie in a single peacock herl and a black hackle of dry-fly quality. When the materials are tied in, wind the thread forward to a position that leaves you enough room for attaching the wing and accommodating a small head.

3. Select two feathers for the wing that are large enough for the size fly being dressed (on left). Remove the soft fibers and fuzz on both of them, making sure that the portion to be used is the same size on both feathers (in middle). Apply some cement on both feathers and superimpose one on top of the other. Hold the exposed stems firmly with your fingers on one hand while you stroke the feathers together by repeatedly drawing them between thumb and first finger on the other hand. This will cement them together and compress the fibers a little at the same time. (Don't make them too slim, or you will ruin the silhouette.) When the cement is dry, trim the feather to length (on right). When tied in, it should reach just barely beyond the hook bend.

4. Divide the top hackle fibers evenly, press them down to each side, and tie in the wing so that it lies flat against the hackle fibers and herl underbody. Adjust the wing so it is parallel with the body before securing it tightly. Cut the surplus stem, wind a small head, and the Black Feather Beetle is finished.

5. The finished Black Feather Beetle.

CRICKETS AND GRASSHOPPERS (ORTHOPTERA)

When most of the important mayfly hatches have come to an end, and the warm summer days of August have slowed fishing activities on the trout stream to the point where only mini-sized artificials seem to work, it used to be customary to hand up the rod and take a swim in the large upstream pool set aside for just such occasions. It was that way until some years ago, when it was discovered that after the mayflies have come and gone, the kickers on grasshoppers and crickets have matured, giving life to the meadow and nearby flatland. Trout are like humans, they have to eat to exist, and as my friend Lefty Kreh says, "A big grasshopper—that's a lot of groceries."

The deer-hair Crickets and Hoppers have proved to be not only good fish-getters, but also very durable; they can stand the repeated punishment that so often destroys other types of flies. The size of flies you will need for a good afternoon of trout fishing is hard to predict, but in the East I have found that a Cricket dressed on a 14 hook is generally a good size. The Hopper should be slightly larger, perhaps dressed on size 8 to 10; but what works in the East may not necessarily work out West on the fast roaring rivers. There, I suspect, they should be quite a bit larger. The best procedure is to collect some specimens when you arrive at your fishing location and match your artificials accordingly.

The method of dressing is the same for both Cricket and Hopper; the difference between them lies in the material color used.

Cricket

Hook	Mustad 94833, size 10 to 14
Thread	Black, prewaxed 6/0
Body	Black fur dubbing
Underwing	Black crow wing quill section tied flat, length of hook
Overwing	Dyed black deer-body hair, slightly longer than underwing
Head	Trimmed hair butts from overwing

Hopper

Hook	Mustad 94833, size 8 to 12
Thread	Yellow, prewaxed 6/0
Body	Yellowish-tan with a touch of olive
Underwing	Brown-mottled turkey-wing quill section, length of hook
Overwing	Natural dun-gray deer body hair, slightly longer than underwing
Head	Trimmed hair butts from overwing
Dubbing Formula	1 part yellow and 1 part tan, with enough medium-olive fur added to give it an olive cast

1. Dub the fur body in the usual manner by rolling the dubbing directly on the waxed tying thread, and wind it on the hook shank like an ordinary dry-fly body. Make sure it is not too skinny. Tie off the dubbing in front and cut the surplus. There must be room enough in front to attach the wing materials and form the deer-hair head.

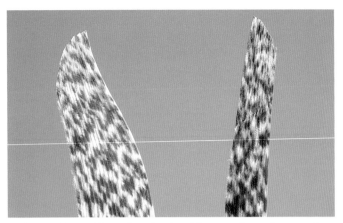

2. Cut a wing quill section that is wide enough to give you the proper width when doubled lengthwise. (Proper width is about three times the body width.) Brush it with tying cement. Double the quill section lengthwise and let it dry before trimming the corners as shown above.

4. Take a bunch of deer body hair and align the tips. Then tie them in on top of the hook. Hold the hair firmly on top; do not allow the hair to spin around the underside. At the most, they can be on each side. While still holding them very tight on top, wind your tying thread through the butt ends on top as well as under the bottom, which is allowed.

3. Lay the wing section flat and parallel over the body and tie it on in front. Cut the surplus and wind over the ends before adding a small amount of clear cement.

5. Trim the head flat on the bottom, then follow by trimming the top and sides as seen. There may be too much hair in the overwing, which can be trimmed away so the butts blend with the rest of the head butts.

RED AND BLACK ANTS

At first I did not intend to include ants in this chapter because I have always felt they deserved a whole book to themselves. Having fished many streams in different parts of the country, I have yet to meet a trout fisherman who didn't treasure a little artificial ant at one time or another. The careless little creatures often venture into tree branches and grass along the stream and, like the rest of the land insects, fall or are blown into the water.

Ants can be dressed in any size you wish, but are generally best in size 14 through 22. Since they are poor swimmers they are not tied as a dry fly, but more like a semi-dry fly that floats half submerged in the surface film. This type of "floating" can be accomplished by trimming the floating hackle top and bottom and letting the side hackle act as legs and prevent it from completely submerging. Whichever you prefer, the red or the black, the ants are dressed by the same method and only the color of the material decides the difference between them. There are times when a wet ant is more productive, and one should certainly carry both wet and dry all the time. To dress a wet ant, the body lumps must be made with tying thread instead of fur. When the two thread lumps are wound they are saturated with clear lacquer, or black enamel. The hackle on the wet dressings need not be dry-fly quality, and a hen hackle of the proper color will do nicely.

Black Ant

Hook	Mustad 94833, size 14 to 22
Thread	Black, prewaxed 6/0
Body	Two black fur lumps, large at the hook bend and smaller in front
Hackle	One rusty-blue dun tied in the middle, dry-fly style, and trimmed top and bottom

Red Ant

Hook	Mustad 94833, size 18 to 22
Thread	Brown, prewaxed 6/0
Body	Two golden-brown fur lumps, large at the hook bend and smaller in front
Hackle	One rusty-blue dun tied in the middle, dry-fly style, and trimmed top and bottom
Dubbing Formula	2 parts medium brown, 1 part chestnut brown, and 1 part yellow

1. Roll some fur on the tying thread and wind it on the hook shank to form the rear lump as seen.

2. Take the tying thread forward and form a smaller lump. Select a hackle and tie it in between the two lumps.

4. Now trim the hackle away on top and bottom, leaving the sides long to act as legs, and the ant imitation is finished.

3. Wind the hackle in regular dry-fly style and tie it off.

5. Front view of the ant. Note the trimmed hackle above and below.

THE CRANE FLY OR DADDY LONG LEGS

In late summer, when most of our regular fly hatches are long gone, we dig deep down in the darkest corners of our fly boxes in search for a taken pattern. Terrestrials might work at times, but there is an insect that is much more appealing to the trout, and that's the crane fly adult, or Daddy Long Legs, as it's called in Europe. My tutor, Bill Blades, insisted, that if the natural insect had legs, why not the artificial? I agree the Daddy Long Legs is much more interesting than an ordinary hackle skater or large variant, and more often than not, it will save the day for you.

Daddy Long Legs

Hook:	Partridge L3B, up eyed dry fly hook, size 10, 12, or 14
Thread	Brown, prewaxed 6/0 or 8/0
Body	Medium brown hackle with fibers reversed and set in tying cement
Legs	6 long fibers from a ringneck pheasant tail knotted
Wings	Two grizzly, grizzly variants, or cree hackle tips
Hackle	One grizzly and one brown hackle, tied dry fly style
Head	Brown tying thread

Note: The body can also me made with yellow or tan hackle.

1. Attach the tying thread and wind it to the middle of the shank.

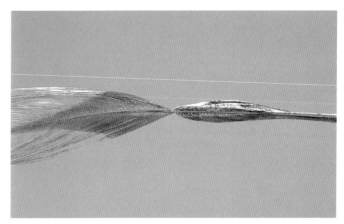

2. Select a large hackle and remove the fuzz from the base. Now stroke down about ³/₄-inch of the fibers on each side of the stem and set them in cement as explained in the dry fly chapter for making the extension body steps 1 through 6. When dry, cut off the excess hackle and trim the body portion so it's one and a half hook length.

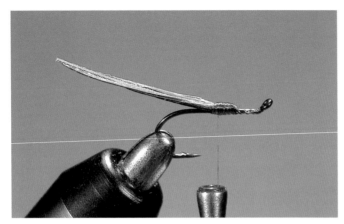

but the procedure is the same. It is best to cut the three fibers for the right side of the body from the right side of the tail stem, and the fibers for the left legs from the other side. This will make them easier to set when tying them in. With a little practice you should have little trouble making the legs. Hold a leg fiber against the mono loop on the near side. The loop should be in the middle of the fiber for the best result.

3. Tie in the body portion in the middle of the hook shank so it sits with a slight upward angle as seen in the photo.

4. To make the legs on the Daddy Long Legs and other flies, I have invented the "Jorgensen leg knotting machine." There are no moving parts, just a simple monofilament loop inserted in the jaws of your vise. The following four steps will show the ease with which one can knot the legs. For illustration, I have used a heavier leg fiber than is used for the Daddy Long Legs,

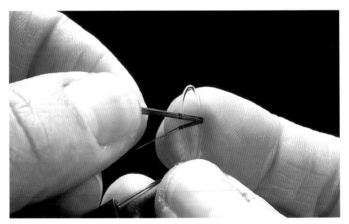

5. Now fold the tip portion of the fiber behind to the left up against the back of the loop. Let the fiber have a slight downward angle.

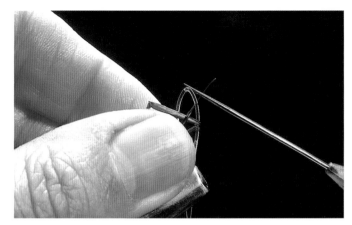

6. Continue to move the fiber tip to the front and against the loop so it points almost straight up. Now pull the fiber tip through the top of the loop with you dubbing needle.

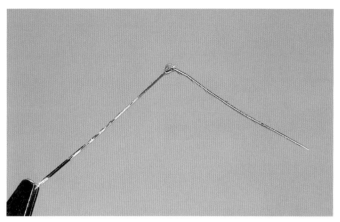

8. The finished leg. You need six legs for the Daddy Long Legs.

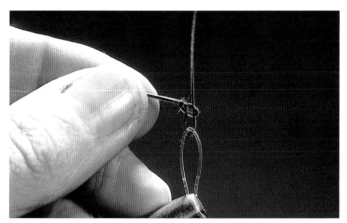

7. Pull the fiber leg off the loop and pull the knot tight. See the finished leg in step 8.

9. Tie in three legs on each side of the body. There is no orderly way to do this. When they are tied in, take a turn of thread close behind each leg to make them sit nicely separated.

10. Select two hackle tips and tie them in so they sit as seen in the photo. I do not strip the stem before I tie them in, but tie directly over the hackle fibers. This gives you better control over the wing position when tying them in. Each wing should be one body length measured from the hook eye to the tip of the extension body. After securing the wings, take a close turn of thread directly behind each wing so they sit at an angle as shown in the photo.

11. Trim the surplus wing material. Now tie in the hackle and wind it dry-fly style to finish the fly.

Selected Patterns

Saabye's Daddy Long Legs

Hook	Mustad 80050BR, size 8 to 12
Thread	Black, prewaxed 12/0
Body	Natural raffia over medium-heavy nylon leader material
Ribbing	Fine oval gold tinsel
Legs	6 fibers from a ringneck pheasant tail, knotted
Wings	Two natural brown hackle tips from a rooster neck
Hackle	Natural brown rooster hackle
Head	Black tying thread

Ed Hewitt's Skater

Hook	Extra-short dry fly hook, size 12 to 16
Thread	Black, prewaxed 8/0
Hackle	Two very stiff, long-fibered spade hackle, wound underside to underside and pressed together
Head	Black tying thread

Chapter 9
Coastal Flies

When I was a little kid living in Denmark I was lucky enough to spend my summer vacation from school at a beach house by the sea with my parents. As soon as I got there I grabbed my shrimp net and waded out and started to scrape the sandy bottom for the little clear sand shrimp I had discovered the year before. I also found some much larger dark shrimp by shaking the seaweed. Now that Denmark has some of the finest sea trout fishing in the world, it stands to reason that some of these little creatures I played with as a kid are a very important food source for the fish. The two patterns that follow are my suggestion for imitating the shrimp.

Sand Shrimp

Hook	Partridge Sea Prince CS52, size 6, 8
Thread	Clear monofilament sewing thread
Eyes	Section of small bead chain
Feelers	Four strands of pearl crystal flash, 1 1/4 hook length
Head	Small bunch of light olive SLF hank, one hook gap long
Body	Light olive SLF dubbing ribbed with clear tying thread
Legs	Body material picked out

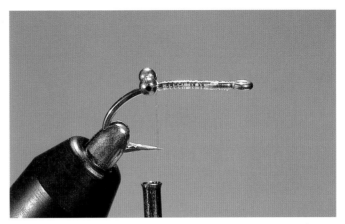

1. Attach the tying thread and fasten the bead eyes securely at a point above midway between the barb and the hook point. Add a little cement if needed.

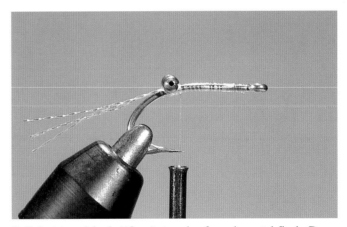

2. Select two 4-inch (10cm) strands of pearl crystal flash. Double them over the tying thread and tie them in behind the bead eyes, then lay them between the eyes and tie them down in front. Trim to length.

3. Select a thin bunch of the hank and tie it in front of the bead eyes with a hook gap section extending out over the crystal flash. Set it at a light downward angle. Do not cut the surplus.

5. Insert the SLF in the loop and spin a tapered robe-like dubbing that is not too tight. Wind the dubbing back to the eyes and tie it off. Cut the surplus material and spiral the tying thread down the body in close turns and tie it off by the hook eye before cutting it.

4. Criss-cross the surplus hank between the bead eyes, tie it down. Trim the surplus and wind the tying thread over the shank close to the eye. Form a 3-inch spinning loop, then hold the tying thread toward the rear and over one of the bead eyes and let it hang by the bobbin. The body can then be wound over the thread and be ready to tie off the body material.

6. Pick out some dubbing under the body with a needle or a piece of velcro in the end of a stick to represent the legs, and your shrimp is finished.

Large Dark Shrimp

This shrimp is very much like the famous General Practitioner salmon fly in appearance, but is smaller and darker overall.

Hook	Partridge traditional Bartleet, single or double, size 2, 4, or 6
Thread	Brown, prewaxed 8/0
Antennae	Large reddish orange breast feather from a golden pheasant wound as a hackle above the barb with fibers projecting past the bend
Head	A small reddish orange breast feather from a golden pheasant
Body	Jorgensen signature SLF dubbing 14, Fall brown, ribbed with brown tying thread
Legs	Body material picked out underneath
Back	Two reddish orange breast feathers from a golden pheasant tied flat
Eyes	Golden pheasant tipped with center trimmed out to form a V shape, lacquered
Head	Brown tying thread

1. Tie in the large reddish orange feather by the tip at a position above the hook point. The fibers on the feather should be about 1 1/2 hook length. Wind it as a wet fly hackle. Tie it off and cut the surplus. Now tie in a small reddish orange feather over the hackle as a head so it sits flat and projects about one hook gap beyond the bend as seen in the picture.

2. Form the body as explained in steps 4, 5, and 6 for tying the Sand shrimp.

3. The eyes are made from a golden pheasant tipped feather (left). The lower fibers have been pulled off and the center trimmed out, leaving a 2mm portion of fibers on each side. Apply a little cement on the tip of each fiber bunch to hold them together. Now prepare a reddish orange breast feather as shown to the right in the photograph. Both the tipped and the breast feather should be long enough to reach a little beyond the bend of the hook, measured from the front of the finished body portion where they will be tied in.

4. Flatten the clear stems a little on both feathers, then tie in the breast feather first so it sits flat over the body and extends a little beyond the bend. Next, tie in the tipped section directly on top with the "eyes" extending a little beyond the bend and the "eyes" projecting out at the same angle on both sides of the hook bend. Trim the surplus feather and add a little head cement on the tie in windings.

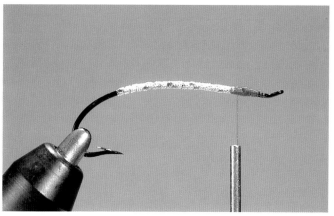

5. Select another reddish orange breast feather and prepare it like the first one. Tie it in flat over the tipped section so it reaches to the end of the hook bend. Cut the surplus feather and wind a smooth head before applying several coats of head cement on the windings. This completes the shrimp.

1. Attach the tying thread and tie in a stand of fine gold tinsel in front, $^3/_{16}$-inch (5mm) from the hook eye. Wind it back to above the hook point, then forward to the tie in spot and tie it off. Trim the surplus.

The Golden Fox

MORTEN VALEUR

Hook	Partridge Traditional Bartleet CS10/1 size 6
Thread	Red, prewaxed 6/0, 8/0
Body	Fine gold tinsel, metal or mylar
First Wing	Sparse bunch of white Arctic fox tail over and under the body, half a hook length past the bend
Second Wing	Sparse bunch of Arctic fox tail dyed golden, reaching to one hook gap past the length of wing number one. Add a few strands of finest silver tinsel over the wing
Hackle	Badger hackle dyed orange
Third Wing	Arctic fox tail dyed olive, slightly longer than wing number two
Beard	Fine Arctic fox body hair dyed red
Head	Red tying thread

2. Tie in the first wing right in front of the body on top and the same amount of hair under the body as seen in the photo.

3. Tie in the second wing in front of the first. Now add the fine tinsel over the wing before winding the hackle in front. Make sure you still have a short space on the shank in front of the hackle for the third wing and red beard.

5. Fold the wing material back over the second wing and tie it down. Now fold the beard hair back and tie it down. Wind a small short head, give it a couple of coats of lacquer and your fly is finished.

4. Measure the wing material and tie it in so it projects out over the hook eye. Cut a sparse bunch of red hair and tie it under the shank pointing in the same direction as the wing material, and long enough to reach to the hook point when folded back. Please note the head space. It reaches from tight against the hook eye to directly in front of the hackle.

Selected Patterns

The Rusty Fox

Poul Jorgensen

Hook	Partridge Traditional Bartleet, CS10/1 size 1/0, 1, 2, 4. or 6
Thread	Red
Body	Embossed silver tinsel
First Wing	Sparse bunch of dark orange Arctic fox tail reaching to the bend
First Hackle	Black, with soft fibers as long as wing and wound directly in front of wing and blending with the wing
Second Wing	Sparse bunch of rusty Arctic fox tail a little longer than the first wing. Add a few strands of finest silver tinsel over the wing
Second Hackle	Purple, with soft fibers slightly longer than the first hackle, and wound directly in front of second wing
Third Wing	Sparse bunch of rusty Arctic fox tail tied in pointing out over the hook eye, then folded back and set as a wing that reaches to a hook gap past the second wing
Third Hackle	Orange, with soft fibers slightly longer than the second, and wound directly in front of and blending with the second hackle
Cheeks	Jungle cock feathers, optional
Head	Red tying thread

The Black Fox

Poul Jorgensen

Hook	Partridge Traditional Bartleet CS10/1, size 1/0, 1, 2, 4, or 6
Thread	Red, prewaxed 6/0, or 8/0
Body	Embossed silver tinsel
First Wing	Sparse bunch of black Arctic fox tail reaching to end of hook bend
First Hackle	Badger dyed red, with soft fibers as long as wing and wound directly in front of wing and blending with the wing
Second Wing	Sparse bunch of black Arctic fox tail a little longer than the first wing. Add a few strands of finest silver tinsel over the wing
Second Hackle	Badger dyed blue, with soft fibers slightly longer than the first hackle, and wound directly in front of second wing
Third Wing	Sparse bunch of black Arctic fox tail tied in pointing out over the hook eye, then folded back and set as a wing that reaches a hook gap past the second wing
Third Hackle	Badger dyed yellow, with soft fibers slightly longer than the second, and wound directly in front of and blending with the second hackle
Cheeks	Jungle cock feathers (optional)
Head	Red tying thread

Martin's Needlefish   MARTIN HEDEGAARD

Tube	Morrum tube with head reversed, about 1³/₄ inches long, including plastic tube
Thread	Red, prewaxed 6/0
Head	Brass part of morrum tube
Underwing	Fine pearl or light blue flash
Overwing	Small bunch of olive SLF hank and a few strands of flash, over which is a small bunch of Arctic fox, dyed tan
Gills	Red tying thread

Note: Because of the brass head and the soft material, this fly is very lively in the water when fished.

Buksetrolden   MARTIN HEDEGAARD

Hook	Mustad 80400BLN, size 4 to 8
Thread	Black, prewaxed 6/0
Tail	Arctic fox body hair, dyed black, and small amount of holographic flash
Body	Black Seal-Ex or SLF #41
Ribbing	Oval silver tinsel
Wing	Black holographic flash, badger body hair dyed orange, over which is a small bunch of Arctic fox hair dyed black
Hackle	Opossum hair spun in a loop and wound as hackle
Head	Black tying thread

Chapter 10
Northern Pike Flies

The first fish I ever caught was a northern pike. My father took me fishing in some small farm pond near my grandfather's country school in Mellemballe on the island of Fyn in Denmark. We started out early in the morning and packed the car with a shoe box full of open face sandwiches with herring, egg, and cheese, which was consumed together with beer and snaps (for the adults in the party that is). The fishing was done with some long cane poles with a reel, and a line fitted with a large red bobber. The live golden shiner was attached to a double pike hook with a braided wire inserted through its skin with a long needle. At the time, as a little kid, it was a lot of fun and I always looked forward to the fishing outings.

Now, as an adult, I still look forward to a fishing outing when pike are on the schedule. I no longer use live bait on a long cane pole, instead I engage in one of the most exciting fly-fishing experiences one can ever ask for—fly-fishing for northern pike with large flies fished under or on the surface.

The flies I have selected for this chapter are but a few of those effective for pike, but as fly tiers, part of the fun is to design some flies yourself and go after the hungry monsters. However, it is inconceivable not to have some 5-inch-long (12.5cm) Lefty's Deceivers in your fly box together with some Hammerhead Frogs. The best colors for the Deceivers are red and white, orange and black, and yellow and black. In addition, you will find Morten Valeur's Orange Pike fly tied on a morrum tube a deadly addition to your selection of pike flies.

THE HAMMERHEAD FROG

The most important factor in the overall scheme of its effectiveness is the keel hook, which allows the angler to cast into Lilly pads and weedy shores and retrieve the bug slowly without hanging up because it stays on the surface with the hook point up. It can also be tied on a regular hook for open water fishing.

The Hammerhead can be dressed in any size and color combination. The important thing is to learn the hair application. As you know, the fish will take a plain gray because it looks like food, while the multa colored one is for the fisherman because it's pretty. But whichever you choose, when a pike takes a hammerhead on the surface, it's like if someone had thrown in a hand grenade.

The Hammerhead Frog

Hook	Mustad stinger hook, 37187 size1/0 to 6, modified or Partridge Bartleet Superior CS10-2, size1/0 to 6
Thread	Strong flat mono cord, any color
Body	Butt ends of leg material wound with tying thread
Legs	Medium bunch of green bucktail, three times the hook length, tied splayed
Head	Two applications of yellow deer body hair under the hook shank, alternate layers of green, yellow, green, on top of the hook shank. All hair trimmed as explained in the instructions.

Note: The Frog is dressed as a medium size fly. For larger flies you should increase the overall length of all the materials. Also, instead of bucktail for the legs, try using long soft hackles with a small hair-bunch in between.

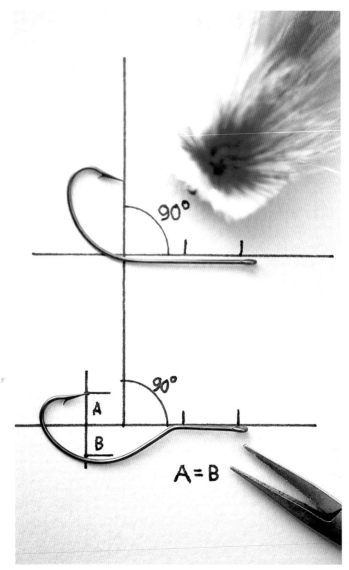

1. Prepare the stinger hook as shown in the photograph.

2. Attach the tying thread and tie in a medium size bunch of green bucktail. Allow a space of a $^1/_4$-inch (about 6mm) bare shank between the butt ends of the bucktail and the hook eye. Fasten it securely with tying thread, then divide the hair into two equal bunches and set splayed with crisscross windings. Also take some windings directly around the base of each bunch. Apply some thin penetrating cement on all thread windings and let dry. Let the tying thread hang directly in front of the butt ends of the leg hair.

3. Cut a bunch of yellow deer body hair that is about 2 inches long (5cm) and is of good "hollow" quality. The quantity of hair should have a diameter like a yellow lead pencil when lightly compressed. Clean out the underfur and hold the hair bunch on top and parallel with the hook shank. There should be about 1 inch (25mm) of hair in front of your fingertips. Now take two loose turns of thread around the hair bunch and hook shank.

4. Hold the hair firmly with your fingers and pull the thread loops tight with a direct down pull flaring it on top of the shank. Do not let it spin.

5. Take an extra turn of thread around the bunch and pull it tight as you twist the hair bunch around so it sits under the shank, with the fibers distributed evenly out to each side. Apply a small amount of Super Glue gel on the tie-in spot.

6. Cut a bunch of green hair and prepare it as explained in step 3. Place it on top of the shank at the same tie-in spot as the yellow hair and hold it while taking two turns of thread around it. Place your thumb against the hair on the far side and hold your index finger on the yellow hair under the shank and pull the thread loops tight. The finger positions will prevent the green hair from being pulled off the top by the torque of the thread, and also prevent the yellow hair from being pulled away from the center. When the hair is set, flatten it with your fingers so the hair is set evenly to the sides. Hold the whole structure flat with your fingers and make sure that the thread windings are pulled completely tight. The small amount of Super Glue gel you applied on the shank and thread windings in step 5 will hold the whole head tight on the shank when it is finished.

7. Turn the fly bottom up and apply another bunch of yellow hair on top of the first. Turn the fly right side up and add, first a yellow bunch over the green, and last, add a green bunch with fibers half as long as the previous layers on top. Make sure all thread windings are pulled tight. Now finish off with some half hitches or whip finish in the middle where the hair is tied in. Apply a small amount of thin cement on the windings.

8. When all the hair is in place, find the eye of the hook and press the hair back so it stands up. The hair is now trimmed as seen in the following steps.

10. Trim even across the front.

9. Trim flat across the bottom.

11. Trim the top high and across.

12. Trim the sides wide.

14. Large Hammerhead fly with hackle legs.

13. Finished frog.

Lefty's Deceiver—Red and White

Hook	Mustad 34007, size 1/0 to 3/0
Thread	Red, strong flat mono cord
Tail	Six to eight large white saddle hackles with a grizzly saddle on each side as long as the tail, on the outside which is six to eight strands of Flashabou each side, as long as the tail
Body	Tying thread from securing the tail hackles
Collar	Arctic fox tail dyed red, tied on the sides and reaching a hook length past the bend
Topping	Silver fox tail dyed vine color, reaching ²/₃ down the tail
Head	Red tying thread

Note: Lefty's original is tied with a bucktail collar. I have taken the liberty of using Arctic fox tail. Sorry Lefty.

2. Select eight white saddle hackles 5 inches long and line up the tips. Trim off some of the fuzz at the base and tie them in together at the bend. Lefty sometimes dipped them in a little water and stroked them together before tying them in to have more control over the feathers. Fasten them securely, then tie in a narrow grizzly hackle on each side. Last, tie in the Flashabou on each side of the tail. You are now ready for the collar.

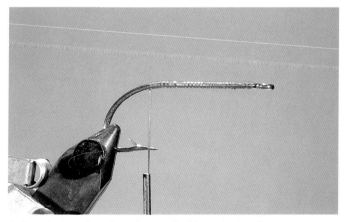

1. Attach the tying thread and wind it to the bend.

3. Tie in a good bunch of red Arctic fox tail in front on each side of the hook. It should be evenly distributed above and below the hook shank as seen in the photo.

Black and Orange Deceiver

Hook	Mustad 37007, size 1/0 to 3/0
Thread	Red, strong flat mono cord
Tail	Six to eight large black saddle hackles with six to eight strands of gold crystal flash on each side
Collar	Arctic fox tail dyed orange and set all around as a collar
Head	Red tying thread

4. Tie in a good bunch of vine colored hair so it sits low enough to blend with the rest of the material. Now wind the head, tie it off and give it several coats of good tying cement, and your deceiver is finished.

Morten's Orange Pike Fly

Tube	Morrum system, 3/4-inch long (20mm)
Thread	Red, prewaxed 6/0 or 8/0
First Wing	Orange Arctic fox tail, two and a half times as long as the tube
Second Wing	Orange Icelandic hair, 5 inches long, (128mm) over which you tie in four to six strands of thin pearl flash
Hackle	Badger dyed orange
Third Wing	Hot orange Icelandic hair, same length as second wing
Sides	Narrow grizzly hackle dyed orange on each side
Head	Red tying thread

Note: The fly can also be tied on a Mustad 37007, size 1/0 to 3/0.

If you have not been involved in salmon fly tying, you may not be familiar with tube flies at all. These flies, however, are not just for salmon, but are being used for many other game fish, including northern pike. To tie tube flies you will need a special vise attachment. The one I use is the HS vise made in Denmark. It comes with three different diameter rods, thus enabling you to tie flies on different diameter tubes, including the Morrum tube used for the fly you are about to tie. There are other vises available, and I suggest you check with your supplier of tools and material who may carry them.

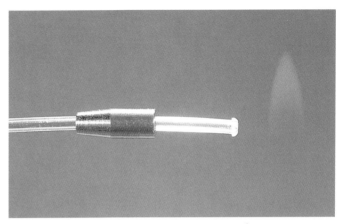

1. The morrum tube comes in two pieces: A 1 1/2-inch (40mm) long thin plastic tube, and a 1/2-inch (10mm) long brass piece that is slightly tapered in one end. Prepare the tube by sliding the brass piece onto the plastic tube, then make a small ridge in the end by lightly warming it with a lighter, thus preventing the brass piece from being pulled off.

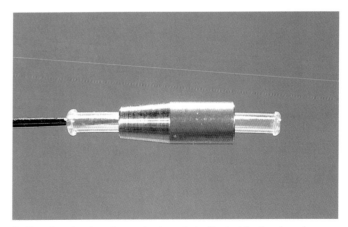

2. Cut the plastic tube to the length indicated in the dressing and form a small ridge like in the other end. The brass piece is now trapped on the tube and cannot be pulled off, the way it was designed to be.

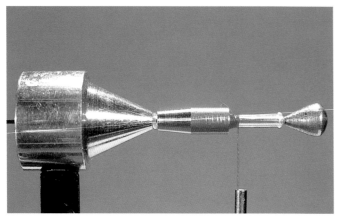

3. Place your favorite tube fly tool in the vise and fasten the tube on the rod as seen in the photo. If you want your hook to be held steady in a small silicone piece, the tapered end of the brass piece should be placed to the left. If the flat end is to the left, the hook will be hanging free when the fly is being fished. As you can see in the photo, I have chosen to use the tapered end for the silicone sleeve to be fitted. Now attach your tying thread and wind it tightly up against the brass piece to hold it in place while keeping the short plastic tube free in front where the fly is going to be tied in.

4. Tie in the first wing directly in front of the brass piece.

5. Select a small bunch of the long Icelandic hair and tie it in over the first wing, over which you tie in the pearl flash that should be as long as the wing. Now tie in a grizzly hackle on each side reaching to near the end of the wing.

6. Tie in the badger hackle by the tip, double the fibers back and wind it as a wet fly hackle. Now tie in the third wing on the remaining space in front so it points out over the hook eye as seen in the photo. Please note the head space. It reaches from tight against the little ridge on the plastic tube to directly in front of the hackle.

8. Silicone hose in end of tube ready for hook to be inserted.

7. Fold the wing back over the second wing and tie it down. Wind the head, give it a couple of coats of lacquer, and your fly is finished.

Selected Patterns

Black Back   Henrik Kure

Hook	Mustad 80300BR, size 2 to 8
Thread	White, prewaxed 6/0
Eyes	Medium-size glass
Tail	Yellow Angel Hair with black/red Angel Hair over
Body	Yellow marabou, yellow Angel Hair, and red marabou spun in a loop and wound as a hackle
Tail/Back	Black rabbit hair strip
Sides	Yellow Krystal Flash
Head	White tying thread

Golden Olive Baitfish   Henrik Kure

Hook	Mustad 80300BR, size 2 to 8
Thread	White, prewaxed 6/0
Eyes	Medium-size glass
Tail	Yellow Angel Hair and grizzly marabou, dyed golden olive
Body	Golden olive marabou wound together with yellow Angel Hair
Tail/Back	Black rabbit hair strip
Sides	Yellow Krystal Flash
Head	White tying thread

Ginger Baitfish   Henrik Kure

Hook	Mustad 80300BR, size 2 to 8
Thread	White, prewaxed 6/0
Eyes	Medium-size glass
Tail	Copper Angel Hair and grizzly marabou, dyed ginger
Body	Grizzly marabou dyed ginger and wound together with copper Angel Hair
Tail/Back	Tan rabbit hair strip
Sides	Brown Krystal Flash
Head	White tying thread

Olive Baitfish   Henrik Kure

Hook	Mustad 80300BR, size 2 to 8
Thread	White, prewaxed 6/0
Eyes	Medium-size glass
Tail	Yellow Angel Hair and grizzly marabou, dyed olive
Body	Grizzly marabou dyed olive and wound with yellow Angel Hair
Tail/Back	Black rabbit hair strip
Sides	Yellow Krystal Flash
Head	White tying thread

Opposite: *Four baitfish pike flies by Henrik Kure.*
Photo by Morten Valeur

Index